American Singularity

In the quest to meet the summit of our potential, it is my firm conviction that our American Constitution will serve future generations with all of their complexities, as it has the current generation and the generations of our forebears.

RICHARD B. RUSSELL

THE RICHARD B. RUSSELL LECTURE SERIES

The Richard B. Russell Foundation and the University of Georgia have joined in establishing this lecture series to honor the late Senator Russell. The Richard B. Russell Lectures will extend through the 1980s, addressing the Bicentennial of the Federal Constitution and encompassing the Charter of the University of Georgia in 1785. The Russell Lectures are scheduled for each year during this decade, at which time a distinguished guest of the University of Georgia will present three addresses on some notable aspect of the Constitution.

Harold M. Hyman

American Singularity

The 1787 Northwest Ordinance, the 1862 Homestead and Morrill Acts, and the 1944 G.I. Bill

THE RICHARD B. RUSSELL LECTURES
NUMBER FIVE

The University of Georgia Press
Athens and London

© 1986 by the University of Georgia Press
Athens, Georgia 30602
All rights reserved

Set in Palatino

The paper in this book meets the guidelines for
permanence and durability of the Committee on
Production Guidelines for Book Longevity of the
Council on Library Resources.

Printed in the United States of America

90 89 88 87 86   5 4 3 2 1

Library of Congress Cataloging in Publication Data

Hyman, Harold M. (Harold Melvin), 1924–
    American singularity.

    (The Richard B. Russell lectures; no.5)
    Includes index.
    1. United States—Public lands—History.   2. School
lands—United States—History.   3. Veterans—Education—
Law and legislation—United States—History.   I. Title.
II. Series.
KF352.H96 1987   343.73'0256   86-7073
ISBN 0-8203-0886-2 (alk. paper)   347.303256

TO REBECCA

who is also first

Contents

Acknowledgments

The invitation to me from the Richard B. Russell Foundation and the University of Georgia historians to be the 1985 Richard B. Russell Lecturer was, and is, a cherished honor. I thank all concerned for the invitation and for the warm hospitality I enjoyed in Athens, both on and off campus. Editor Karen Orchard and Ellen Harris of the University of Georgia Press, copy editor Kathleen B. Durham, and my Rice University secretary and friend Sylvia Ross bore heavy burdens in transforming the typescript of the lectures into a readable form, and I greatly appreciate their patience and sharp eyes. Thanks too to Rice University doctoral candidates Kenneth DeVille and Charles Zelden who dug diligently through the holdings of the Fondren Library at Rice, and to the very helpful and efficient library staff at Rice, especially Ferne B. Hyman, who kept opening windows to worlds new to me.

New worlds are refreshing, especially after three-plus decades of trying to understand diverse aspects of our federally arranged, constitutionally limited, politically democratic, and economically capitalistic constitutional and legal system. During that third of a century, I attended little, however, to the history of public higher education and of changing universes of learning, as measures of Americans' rights. Then in 1983, Dr. Patricia Breivik, director of the Auraria Library, Denver, invited me to give the keynote address at a Colorado conference on technology and learning. In my research, I "discovered" a fascinating area of American history, one new to me but linked to my ongoing concerns about legal-constitutional history. My paper at this constructive Colorado conference centered on interactions between public institutions of higher learning and research scholarship—interactions deriving from explosions of knowl-

Acknowledgments

edge and of data retrieval technologies. I had learned, as examples, that the steam printing press (ca. 1814) and the card catalog (ca. 1880s) were as stimulating and troubling to contemporary data-retrieving librarians and research academics as the computer in the 1970s and 1980s.[1]

I take this opportunity to thank Dr. Breivik and her colleagues for the opportunity they afforded me to consider these matters. As research tends to do, that inquiry suggested others, especially the question of access as a matter of right to the public colleges and universities that became major contexts for learning and technology. My interest broadened further to public policies on access to land or equivalent property and to legal remedies for all rights. When the invitation from the Russell Foundation arrived, I was wondering if what I understood about Americans' access to land, learning, and law formed part of a singular American historical experience.

Perhaps the question of what makes our history exceptional, if indeed it is, will elevate sights for the bicentennial of the Constitution above that of a certain book publisher of 1875. He, as the centennial of the Revolution neared, encouraged the writing of an American history because, as the intended author, Martha J. Lamb, confided to Chief Justice of the United States Morrison R. Waite, it "cannot fail to sell, particularly in this centennial hubbub." Indeed, her publisher was giving top priority to her history "in order to catch the centennial penny."[2] What follows has different goals.

American Singularity

Introduction

America, Goethe wrote almost two hundred years ago, *"du hast es besser."* America, insisted my Rice University colleague, historian Allen Matusow, no longer has it better. Instead, he suggested in his important 1984 book on the quality of American liberalism in the 1960s, this society is unraveling.[1]

Not so, assert more optimistic historians Peter Clelak and William Chafe who argue in their recent books that, though America's problems and frustrations were recurring and tenacious and divisions profound, the decades since 1945 were marked by high aspirations and achievements for social justice and individual fulfillment. Sometimes progress has been stunning, they conclude about America's unfinished journey into the present.

Choruses from the Critical Legal Studies left and from the neoconservative right call for poxes on all these houses. In one 1985 meeting, as an example, Norman Podhoretz denounced the new "treason of the intellectuals," and on another occasion Wellesley sociologist Brigitte Berger deplored the "general ideological constellation that is antagonistic to basic American institutions, notably those of capitalism and bourgeois culture, and therefore is almost instinctively sympathetic to socialist . . . alternatives." Saul Bellow, speaking at the stormy ideological battleground of the 1986 PEN conference, stated that "alienation is something to which American writers sometimes have 'a fatuous attachment' . . .[and] the American middle class has been preoccupied with 'common sense desires' such as clothing, shelter, and health care."[2]

Acrimony in academe sinks me into what Lynn White, Jr., called "intellectual gloom," a gloom deepened because this is the season of our Constitution's bicentennial and of the modern

British Constitution's tricentennial deriving from the Glorious Revolution of 1688–89.[3] Can we commemorate them appropriately in an everyman's land of invective? When epithets or labels fly, I usually find myself in a mugwumpy middle.[4] Goethe's frequently quoted perception of the exceptional, even singular good fortune of America, if it is accurate, would raise me up from this depression. Avoiding labelers on my right and left, I ask: Is Matusow correct, or is Goethe?

Before choosing, some contextual concerns deserve attention. We all wear several hats. Matusow and I share those of fellow citizens, fellow historians, and campus colleagues. I wear a bonnet, colored geriatric grey, which he is not yet privileged to don. Many aging academics who also wear it were beneficiaries, supporters, and even initiators or implementers of New Deal welfare and reform policies. Does their presence on faculties substantiate Matusow's thesis that the recent history of America has climaxed in failed reform policies, many of New Deal origins?

To ask the question is to assume that generation gaps exist and that historians are subject to them. One highly visible generation gap among scholars, one perhaps even wider than the present chasm, involved the meaning of war in American history, a topic high among the concerns of members of the American Historical Association assembled for their 1950 national meeting. It was barely five years after the total military victory of World War II and only months after the spectacularly visible (on the new medium, television), technologically exciting, and almost bloodless paramilitary airlift that stymied the Soviet blockade of West Berlin. The frustrations of Korea, Vietnam, and Lebanon for America were in the future.

For historians in 1950, the image of war should be positive not negative, the noted Harvard historian, World War II admiral, and new AHA president, Samuel Eliot Morison, argued in his able, sometimes stirring presidential address. "War," he stated, "does accomplish something. . . . War is better than servitude. . . .

War has been an inescapable part of human history."[5] Morison aimed his argument shrewdly. His audience was obviously generationally divided. A prominent older contingent consisted of persons whose careers predated World War II. Almost without exception, these seniors in the profession were male WASPs who had been intellectually nurtured in a tradition of "revisionist" historianship concerning America's wars produced since the early 1920s by such giants as Charles Beard, Avery Craven, and James G. Randall.[6] Taken together, their work on the purposes of the framers of the Constitution, on the causes and results of the Civil War and Reconstruction, and on Franklin Roosevelt's diplomacy that culminated in Japan attacking Pearl Harbor implied that social, racial, or other betterments were incidental spinoffs or cloaks for manipulative and predatory economic interests.[7]

Morison, wishing to question this tradition, argued that serious historical research could and should proceed on the bases of more neutral assumptions about wars in the history of America. And he implied that America's martial history was less sordid than that of other nations—was, in short, singular.

Morison's target at the 1950 AHA meeting was the large number of younger practitioners crowding the auditorium. In addition to their obvious relative youth, this group dressed less formally than the prewar professoriat, frequently in odd pieces of military clothing. Name tags revealed the non-WASP, eastern and southern European origins of many attendees. Before World War II, few such exotics had penetrated WASP academic preserves. Now the AHA audience included numerous Catholics and Jews, a few Negroes and Asians, and a tiny number of non-spouse white women.

An academic revolution was occurring, one resulting largely from the democratizing impacts of World War II on American higher education, especially the effects of the 1944 G.I. Bill which subsidized the educations of the great majority of World War II veterans in Morison's audience. Few among them attended the Ivy League colleges and graduate schools that had all but monopolized professional preparation until World War II. Instead, most graduated from non-Ivy state schools and land-grant universities, including those developed under the 1787 Northwest Ordinance and the 1862 Morrill Act.[8]

Morison believed that these younger historians could balance professional training with their personal experiences in the recent global war. He shared with veterans a sense that they had been neither credulous dupes engaged in fools' errands nor lackeys of sinister yet vague and impersonal economic forces, but rather participants in a necessary and proper crusade against consummate evils. Likening the World War II crusaders to Oliver Wendell Holmes's Civil War generation, which Holmes had written was "touched with fire" in service to the nation, Morison advised these "young intellectuals" to reconsider the martial history of the nation in a nondebunking spirit. Decrying the hypercritical approach, as he described it, of his own, older, strongly revisionist peers, Morison insisted revisionism should give way in part because holders of the attitude "ignored wars, belittled wars [and] taught that no war was necessary and no war did any good, even to the victor." No more. Fascism proved that overwhelming evils existed and that such evils justified wars waged to uproot them. Historians were going to study America's wars some more, and respectfully this time, Morison concluded.[9]

"Admiral" Morison's navigation between the rocks of the wars of America and the shoals of historians' attitudes toward wars did forecast and perhaps inspired significant reconsiderations of America's wars and of the 1787 Constitution in particular and of American history in general. His position that not all wars were useless, conspiratorially contrived, and evil in consequences made sense to many of these neophyte historians whose generation had so recently achieved the military success against fascism. To be sure, then and since, historians properly respected

Beard's, Craven's, and Randall's writings. But in ways that likely gratified Morison, many of the then-younger historians substantially modified the revisionist giants' skeptical approaches to the history of American wars. Many "re-revisionist" histories of American wars retain Morison's guardedly optimistic conclusions about progress even during wars.[10]

But now, a third of a century after 1950, the pendulum is returning, or has returned, to something like the Beardian revisionist positions. Now the young World War II veterans of 1950 are the profession's creaky seniors. And in one of history's wry jests, many present juniors in the profession are, in effect, voting with their research notes and word processors against Morison and for essentially Beardian views. A generation gap is growing, not "only" about wars in our history but about what our wars did to our history. It is a gap on one side of which, to simplify greatly, many present oldsters share Goethe's (and Morison's) assumptions and conclusions. On the other side of the gap, many younger, social science–minded, "new" political and social historians and history-minded social scientists tend like Matusow toward pessimistic deconstructionism.

Perhaps, in light of the rush to social-science methods and judgments, we should echo W. H. Auden's admonition: "Thou shalt not sit / With statisticians nor commit a social science." But though greyheads mutter and poets nag, no historian can wisely ignore the rich, diverse research worlds talented younger colleagues are opening, or their accumulating conclusions that liberalism, democracy, and capitalism are losing ground or are already bankrupt throughout the western world but especially in America.[11]

The volume and tone of these anticipatory obsequies moved Christopher Lasch to suggest recently that we are swimming, or drowning, in a rhetoric of national, social, and individual failure. Producers of this rhetoric, he continued, are so filled with narcissistic self-doubts as to depict America's many adversities and frustrations as impending apocalypses or Auschwitzian holocausts. Peter Parish, an Englishman of the Bryce-Brogan-Brock tradition, said recently that, although Americans have themselves been eroding their ancient devotion to the task of highlighting American singularity, many foreign students of our history still judge the American story as one principally of success. No responsible historian advocates insensitivity to America's historical warts, present difficulties, and perceivable future problems, he continued. Attention must obviously be paid to a nation's dynamics of decline if this is what afflicts us. But attention does not require accepting an assumption that America's reverses or unfulfilled goals are equivalent to total failures or disasters, or that America, if not uniquely blessed, is uniquely cursed for her allegedly singular sins.[12]

Certainly no scholar advocates a return to uncritical "God sheds His grace on thee" approaches of preprofessional historians. One hundred fifty years ago, one such chronicler, George Bancroft, helped to shape the Ages of Jackson and Lincoln by creating a durable if unsophisticated mainstream tradition of a singular, even divinely blessed American history. In Bancroft's idealized story, this exceptional society was virtually free of those encrusted obstructions to individuals' progress that marked, and marred, old Europe. Bancroft's estimates were widely echoed in his time by unsystematic yet important commentators, including the guardians of traditional values who wrote and selected school textbooks and who, one way or another, boiled down the qualities of American singularity to include democracy, opportunity, progress, and pluralism.[13]

Doubters always existed. Then, in the populist-progressive decades, revisionist historians of Morison's concern increasingly challenged Bancroft's star-spangled vision of a happy republic. These professionals, dismissing Bancroft as a credulous and uncritical superpatriotic penman who enshrined the giants of the

Revolution and the framers of the Constitution in his pages, redirected half a dozen disciplines toward more systematic research methods and skeptical attitudes.[14] By 1950, Morison asserted, their enduring, profound revisions of the Bancroft tradition had themselves become blocks to alternative interpretations.[15]

But even the revisionists' monumental and enduring attacks pale in contrast to onslaughts of the past twenty years. "New" political-social-intellectual historians, armed with impressive methodologies, are advancing beyond "progressive" and "consensus" standards of historical criticism to heavily negativistic positions. The newer scholarship has emphasized the existence here of class and of class conflict, of corruption and bias in law and administration, and of economic and production patterns, essentially like those of western Europe.[16]

According to James McPherson of Princeton, one result is that the very "notion of American Exceptionalism has received quite a drubbing" and even suffered "heavy and perhaps irreparable damage." Consensus scholars, he continued, had long asserted that valid proofs of American singularity included material abundance, "free land on the frontier, the absence of a feudal past, exceptional mobility . . . the relative lack of class conflict, . . . [and] the pragmatic and consensual liberalism of our politics." These blessings "set the American people apart from the rest of mankind."[17]

Surveying these shifts in scholars' attitudes, perceptions, and emphases away from a view of a happy American singularity, Parish deplored this new American history, so "replete with injustices, inequalities, and exploitation." He feared that general readers of this recent literature, unaware of alternative modes of research and analysis, see only polar choices between the naive Bancroft tradition or the hypercritical postconsensus interpreters, between "national self-glorification or self-abasement, [between] wrapping one's history in the Stars and Stripes or clothing it in sackcloth and ashes." Such opposed options, he worried, are "not conducive to the ultimate good health of American historiography," and he warned that "to proclaim as the main lesson of American history that if the United States is not the best country in the world it must certainly be the worst is a peculiarly perverted and self-indulgent argument for American exceptionalism,—for the uniqueness of the American experience."[18]

Central in this argument is the question of the historical autonomy, exceptionalism, and singularity of America. Many able analysts have advanced brave hypotheses on both sides of this matter. Side-taking concerning important questions is a habit among historians extending back to man's unwilling exit from Eden—an event that established history as the second oldest profession in the world. Early historians, as well as more recent ones, became, if not advocates, at least moral critics sitting in judgment on significant phenomena. This judgmental stance is perhaps inescapable and desirable. As John Higham concluded, some matters *are* beyond consensus. Historians must be moral critics in order to "rise above a constricting present," and "by the amplitude of their commitment, [to] enter a living past."[19]

Agreed. No canons of sound historical practice with which I am familiar mitigate against strong positions about events, institutions, and individuals, except, perhaps, that historians reaching them should take special pains to stand aloof from the past, else extra hazards exist. As an example of these hazards, in 1885, just when the tiny but growing tribe of professional historians formed the American Historical Association partially to encourage more critical scholarship, Lincoln's former secretaries John Nicolay and John Hay were undertaking their history of the murdered president. Hay advised his colleague: "We must not write a stump speech. . . . We will not fall in with the present tone of blubbering sentiment [about Lincoln], of course. But we ought to write the history of those times like two everlasting angels who know everything, judge everything, and don't care a twang of the harps about one side or the other. . . . [L]et us look upon men as insects and not blame the black beetle because he is not a grasshopper." But, continuing, Hay stipulated one exception to these ascending standards: "We are Lincoln men through and through."[20]

A historian should not be anyone's person "through and through." W. B. Yeats observed that out of quarrels with ourselves we make poetry (and, I hope, history); from our quarrels with others, rhetoric. Scholarship, including historical scholarship, must feed on both, else every campus is a monument to futility. Scholars have every right to reach polar views but, as with Matusow, only after careful research and deliberate weighing of alternative interpretations. Anything less can lead to unprovable judgments which themselves may derive from ideological prejudgments about the past that can shape conclusions in advance of research.[21] By contrast, the eschewing of ideology keeps open alternatives to the Bancroftian optimistic adoration of the American myth and the pessimistic flagellation of this nation's history that Lasch lashed and Parish deplored.

These alternatives rest on middle grounds of interpretation concerning the quality of America's performance as a society and the singularity of its history. Reasonable hopes of recreating limited aspects of the past are better served by steering clear of what Oscar Handlin described as "vast panoramic . . . aspirations to be that transcendental eyeball." The historian, Handlin continued, "in the waking hours . . . must return to the note cards and the tyranny of intractible facts."[22]

Obedience to this happy tyrant can lead toward reasonable objectivity, that recurring concern of historical scholarship. Like newlyweds defining love, objectivity so eludes neat definitions as to remind one of Lincoln's despair at the efforts of his generation to define the legal status of a defeated seceded state: "vain and profitless," "a merely pernicious abstraction," a "metaphysical question and one unnecessary to be forced into discussion."[23] Concerning objectivity, Charles Beard told us that written history remains an act of faith, and Carl Degler reminded us recently that we are always "remaking American history."[24]

In that remaking, skeptical mugwumpery may be a useful approach to reasonable objectivity, a desirable alternative to ideology, and a realistic bypass around the outmoded Bancroft glorification of the singular virtues of America and the contrary school of thought now prevailing among some American historians. By training and perhaps by nature, mugwumps tend to hesitate before abandoning complex but strong relativistic perches in favor of simpler but basically less stable overextended branches. In historiographical if not ornithological terms, I fly in mugwumpy manner between Matusow's estimate about the unraveling of America and Goethe's much-quoted judgment about America having it better, and wonder as I proceed, better in what?

Better in the diffusion of equality before law? Perhaps. But Professor J. R. Pole, the first Russell lecturer, noted in his Jefferson Memorial Lecture at Berkeley that concepts like equality also face historians with exceedingly difficult and delicate analytical tasks.[25] To use another of Lincoln's usable phrases, a "good ready" is now in order, one that allows us to ease that task. Perhaps a rough measure of equality exists in public policies that increased or diminished access to recognized avenues of mobility, opportunity, and success. Such an inquiry, however preliminary, may help to advance the argument concerning access or obstructions and to clarify assertions about America's singularity.

Time and space limitations allow approaches to only a few of these aspects of access. They are access to land, to education, and to legal remedies. I hope to touch on these three measures of access in three time periods: that of the founding of the nation and the creation and early implementation of the Constitution, centering on the 1787 Northwest Ordinance; that of the Civil War and Reconstruction, centering on the 1862 Morrill and Homestead Acts; and that of World War II–present, centering on the 1944 G.I. Bill. This double triad may bring us to a tentative conclusion that the thesis of American singularity or exceptionalism is or is not a busted superstition suitable only for the trash heap of history.

It is the burden of the following pages that these statutes, each in its context, built a linked and consistent access agenda, one unique in the world to my knowledge, at least with respect to the policies sketched. Happily, I am on a small wave of the present in arguing for American exceptionality, for the position is again gaining some academic currency. At this writing, however, the necessary detailed studies of access in the United States and in other nations that would allow confident conclusions have yet to surface.[26] Thirty years ago, Karl Deutsch pleaded for such comparative inquiries, writing that awareness of recurring patterns of the political and social integration of nations was "essential to the pursuit of knowledge." Continuing, Deutsch insisted that "such recurrent patterns of integration, like other relative uniformities in history, raise the problem of comparability or uniqueness of historical events. . . . No historical or political analysis can be written without the use of general concepts in which some notions of uniformity are necessarily implied."[27]

Agreed. Law, especially public law, analyzed comparatively and historically rather than adversarially, and with due sensitivity to the idiosyncratic qualities of each nation surveyed, does offer "general concepts in which some notions of uniformity are necessarily implied." As noted, however, a regretably small number of comparative access studies have come into print since Deutsch's time.[28] Even this slim corpus is of limited use because it has generally taken the form of narrow reports on such subjects as veterans' pensions.[29] A richer but still sparse comparative scholarly literature exists on the histories of education and of frontiers, especially, concerning the latter, in the United States, Canada, and Australia.[30]

Of course it is possible simply to reject history as past, which is obvious, and useless, which is not. Our major historical figures have, thankfully, rarely descended to rejectionism. In December 1862, in the darkest moments of the Civil War, a time when no lights cheered the end of any Union tunnel, Lincoln told the Congress that "the dogmas of the quiet past are inadequate for the stormy present." But only one year later Lincoln had again found "our main reliance" in the war powers of the Constitution, itself a "dogma of the quiet past." Living history—the Constitution—sustained all the extraordinary responses to overt disloyalty and state secessions for which his administration carved a permanent niche in history, responses including the military emancipation of slaves and the military reconstructions of entire states.[31]

This perception of the Constitution as living history bound by its own context, needs, and aims, not ours, is unalluring today, whether on the Reagan right or the Critical Legal Studies left (if that is what the latter is). As an example, in 1982 legal philosopher Michael Perry interred old chestnuts among research subjects, including that most perennially attractive and elusive one in jurisprudence and constitutional history, the intentions of the framers of 1787. "I prefer to let the framers sleep," Perry wrote.[32]

Not I. Like Hamlet, some persons rob themselves of sleep by pursuing endlessly certain undying questions to which final solutions may not soon emerge. Scholars and politicians disinter their *corpora*, as, for example, U.S. Attorney General Edwin Meese III did recently in calling for a return to the "intent of the framers in judging public policies." On that, Supreme Court Justice William J. Brennan, Jr., reflected publicly and accurately (*New York Times* [Oct. 13, 1985], 1) that lawyers and judges have been and are poor historians, that historians and other specialists themselves disagree on this bedrock matter of the framers' intentions, that the contemporary sources are sparse and disputable, and that historians and lawyers ignore the actual contexts of the framing of the Constitution and subsequent developments only at the risk of impoverishing their analyses (though they may win particular court decisions and even elections).

Considering recent obituaries of old comrades among historians, I choose not to wait for the results of comparative research that Karl Deutsch called for so long ago. Instead, I assume that the present reassertion of American exceptionalism is part of a healing process among scholars who, as Thomas Bender suggested recently, are making history whole again, or at least trying to do so.

Historians [Bender continued], to whom we once confidently entrusted the custody of our public memory of ourselves as a nation, have been unable to pull together the vast mountain of scholarship produced in the past quarter century and make of it a coherent and explanatory account of American life. Both readers and writers have been drawn or directed, by a variety of social and cultural mechanisms, to histories of their chosen or inherited group. It is a phenomenon that may represent a disintegration of the civic sense as much as purely intellectual trends in historiography.[33]

And so, with wholeness as aspiration, to the American Revolution scene, the essential context of the 1787 Northwest Ordinance.

In his first Russell lecture, Professor J. R. Pole asserted that Americans received many of their ideas and practices on government and law as pre-Revolutionary gifts from England. Therefore, by extension to the present argument, the late-eighteenth-century experience of America was less singular than derivative.[34] Henry Steele Commager, one of America's preeminent constitutional historians, though not wholly at odds with this view, after examining the sources of American good fortune concerning forms of government and their underlying social values, concluded that they were more domestic than imported. Long before the Revolution, Commager judged, American colonists developed not only constitutional principles but also derivative governing practices that, with egregious exceptions centering on slaveholding, harmonized with many "Enlightenment" theories of privileged Europeans and Englishmen who, in lush salons, debated heavenly cities for eighteenth-century philosophers and other theorists to ponder but not actually to shape. But, Commager concluded, Americans did more than theorize. They created "empires of reason" that not only imagined their heavenly city on earth, but, however partially and imperfectly, institutionalized it by creating rationalized governmental institutions and legal relationships that justify a verdict favoring Americans' singularity in this period. Even before the Revolution, and, most remarkably, during and after it, Americans actually institutionalized standards and procedures in the dozen new and/or substantially revised states' constitutions that came into being, and in the federal Constitution of 1787. National and state constitution-making was among Americans' first great inventions in public law. Resulting constitutions aided Americans to keep what, in large measure, they already possessed before the Stamp Act and its consequences: politically responsible, federally arranged governments that majorities could bend toward improving citizens' access to the sources of life, liberty, and the pursuit of happiness. These constitutions adequately reflected federalism, those layered echelons of locality, state, and nation that the leaders of British governments of the 1760s and 1770s failed, despite their Oxbridge sophistication, adequately to perceive much less accommodate.[35]

American voters and representatives imposed on their new

governments this preeminent duty: to provide nondisadvan-
taged citizens with access to the extremely limited stock of public
assets. These assets were, commonly, land, legal remedies, and,
at least in some states and localities, education.[36]

To counter, Pole's emphasis on a derivative America appears
also to enjoy substantiation by evidence drawn not from the governmental forms that so intrigue him and Commager, but rather
from the subject that so concerned Samuel Eliot Morison, the
conduct and results of war.

Nothing was more important to a society like that of the self-
proclaimed United States in the 1770s than its organization for
war. And in this matter Pole appears to win a point. America's
chosen style of carrying on its Revolution by 1781 became as
unsingular and derivative as Americans could manage. As soon
and as far as possible, Revolutionary Americans Europeanized
their Continental forces from top to bottom. At the top, Lafayette,
Von Steuben, and Kosciusko moved in circles close to Washington. Near the bottom, Von Heer's provost marshal detachment
popularized, among officers at least, Prussian- and French-style
military law and discipline and close-order drill. The influence
of these foreign volunteer officers encouraged the Continental
Congress gradually to bypass localistic "minute man" units and
to minimize state militias in favor of better-disciplined national
forces.

This evolution of military organization in a locality-focused
revolutionary society became politically plausible only because
many Americans shared the European assumption that "laws of
war," like all other "natural laws," existed as self-evident truths.
A common argument of the "Continentals" was that disciplined
national forces would better obey the natural laws of war. That
such ideas about war were common also across the Atlantic is
suggested by the interchangeability of military art of the sort
that today fills museums and senior officers' messes on two con-
tinents. In these idealized depictions of warfare, precisely

aligned ranks of splendidly uniformed, long-term mercenary soldiers maneuver eternally with regimental and dynastic colors uncased, musicians setting cadences, and officers nobly posturing. If weapons killed and maimed men and mounts, the casualties bled little and stunk not at all. Civilians' persons and property are affected by misadventure not scorched earth or genocide policies. The artists proclaim that somehow even war had become civilized.

Wordsmen agreed. Contemporary political theorists including Jean Jacques Burlamaqui, Henry de Jomini, Charles de Montesquieu, and Emmerich de Vattel one way or another fed this "limited war mentality." The prevalence of shared views on both sides of the Atlantic concerning the conduct of war—even of a civil, revolutionary war—is suggested also by the fact that the American Revolution was conducted less bestially than the wars of the Reformation and Counter-Reformation and the imperial-dynastic conflicts that shaped the sixteenth through mid-eighteenth centuries. An exciting sense of progress grew out of the apparent reduction of warfare to a "science" from its former unpredictable and unconstrainable characteristics. War, it seemed, had become more a chess game than a catastrophe; a continuation of politics by other means, theorist Karl von Clausewitz was soon to write.[37] All of which suggests that during their Revolution Americans derived from across the Atlantic their views on the nature and conduct of war.[38]

If Pole appears to be ahead on the issue of war, and, therefore, of American unsingularity, Commager scores on the point of Americans' singular institutionalizations of Enlightenment assumptions. Is he to score again on the alleged exceptionality of Americans' access to land, education, and legal remedies as evidence of implementations of Enlightenment ideas on limiting government and on enhancing individuals' practical rights? More detailed looks at ways that Americans in the 1780–1800 decades, in the Civil War and Reconstruction, and in the post–World War II years exhibited their singularity, or lack of it, by defining access to land, education, and legal remedies may provide useful approaches to answers. Perhaps, too, Goethe's estimate, *"Amerika, du hast es besser,"* and modern scholars' contradicting views can be better resolved.

Chapter 1

The 1787 Northwest Ordinance

James McPherson of Princeton asserted recently, as noted earlier, that the notion of a singular American history has "received quite a drubbing since the heyday of the consensus school of historians in the 1950s, . . . suffering heavy and perhaps irreparable damage." This singularity notion involved an assumption, McPherson stated, "that something special [in] the American experience—whether it was abundance, free land on the frontier, the absence of a feudal past, exceptional mobility and the relative lack of class conflict, or the pragmatic and consensual liberalism of our politics—set the American people apart from the rest of mankind. Historians writing since the 1950s, by contrast, have demonstrated the existence of class and class conflict, ideological politics, land speculation, and patterns of economic and industrial development similar to those of Western Europe which placed the United States in the mainstream of modern North Atlantic history, not on a special and privileged fringe."[1]

Exceptionalist ideas had withered in part as revisionist historians argued that the 1787 Northwest Ordinance and Constitution were conservative, almost counter-revolutionary triumphs more than libertarian achievements. Merrill Jensen, a scholar of great talent and happy longevity, concluded in 1950 that Jefferson's Ordinance of 1784, which the 1787 Northwest Ordinance statute replaced, had "provided for democratic self-government of western territories, and for that reason it was abolished in

1787 by . . . land speculators."[2] Jensen's version won lasting acceptance on and off campuses. Prominent historians discounted contemporary testimonies to the global uniqueness and salutary effects of the 1787 Ordinance, including those by Daniel Webster, who had doubted "whether one single law of any lawgiver, ancient or modern, has produced effects of a more distinct, marked, and lasting character than the Ordinance of 1787," and by Salmon Portland Chase, who had estimated that:

> Never, probably, in the history of the world did . . . legislation fulfill and yet so mightly exceed the expectations of the legislators. The [Northwest] ordinance has been well described as having been a pillar of cloud by day and of fire by night in the settlement and government of the Northwest States. When the settlers went into the wilderness they found the law already there. . . . The purchaser of land became, by that act, a party to the compact, and bound by its perpetual covenants, so far as its conditions did not conflict with the terms of the cessions of the States.[3]

Instead scholars who stressed inequalities in sizes of holdings developed out of the abundant western land concluded that the system of distribution was itself flawed; that, as Vernon Carstensen described it, a "wide gap . . . existed between high intentions and low performance." An outstanding specialist in land history, Carstensen noted that "the history of the public lands has been full of words such as speculators, land monopolists, rings, corrupt officials, hush money, fraudulent entry, land sharks . . . land grabs, . . . mineral grabs, . . . [and] timber grabs." All, Carstensen continued, "excite great interest and bring forth lamentations." But he concluded also that land history was not solely a rogue's gallery: "The alienation of the public land exhibits much human cunning and avarice, but in many instances what was called fraud represented local accommodation to the rigidities and irrelevance of the laws." Honest land seekers by the millions "got their land without violating either the spirit or the letter of the law."[4]

Carstensen's effort the better to balance opposed views is part of an impressive current revival of exceptionalist reinterpretations of the 1787 Northwest Ordinance, along with such related statutes as the 1785 Land Ordinance, the 1789 Judiciary Act, and the Constitution itself. Some of these reexaminers concur that the framers and implementers of the 1787 Constitution and Northwest Ordinance were not merely knavish members of a small, economically self-serving class looking primarily toward a bigger common market. They were, rather, politically pragmatic activists who added to self-interest a desire to make the new nation work and to realize potentialities in the human condition. For these reasons, the framers of the Northwest Ordinance, years before the Bill of Rights graced the Constitution, increased individuals' access to ownership of land, subsidized public education, and stabilized property rights in the territories as preconditions to the enhancement of liberty. They institutionalized the pursuit of happiness by dramatically and singularly enlarging individuals' access to landed property, to education, and to legal remedies for securing rights.[5]

Like Carstensen, Ray Allen Billington acknowledged defects in the ordinance, especially its property qualifications for voting and officeholding and the absolute veto power of the territorial governor in the initial phases of settlement. Nevertheless, Billington concluded that "despite these faults the Ordinance of 1787 did more to save the union than any document save the Constitution. Men could now leave the older states assured that they were not surrendering their [legal protections and ultimate] political privileges." The popular undergraduate history textbook by Bernard Bailyn et al. described the ordinance as solving "at a stroke the problem of relating 'colonies' or dependencies to the central government that Great Britain had been unable to solve." Elsewhere, Bailyn praised the ordinance's "brilliantly imaginative provisions [Article V] made for opening up new lands in the West and for settling new governments within them" as precisely reflecting the optimistic striving mood and interests of almost all white Americans. This concept—no, practice—of equality of new states with older ones, as a statutory procedure triggered by a specified population minimum that transformed settlements into states, was indeed new in history, another American invention in public law equaling the exhilarating state constitution-making of 1775 through 1787. Edmund Morgan saw the ordinance as an early model of how Congress could implement vague clauses of the new Constitution.[6] Peter Onuf, whose monographic output on all these matters is itself a cottage industry, asserted recently that "Americans would continue to celebrate the Northwest Ordinance, both for what it had accomplished in the early history of the territorial system and for the enlightened principles it set forth."[7]

Such positive estimates of the 1787 Ordinance echo James Monroe's, who assured Jefferson the 1787 version retained "the most important principles" of the superseded law of 1784.[8] Robert Berkhofer concluded that the two men did indeed share in a consensus of the 1780s that they were providing for the expansion of a republican empire; that "this [American] empire was *novus ordo sceclorum*, as they proudly proclaimed on their Great Seal; [and that] the United States was not only a newly-independent nation but a new type of nation." New in what? "Its . . . republican institutions," Berkhofer continued, including "religious freedom, relative, economic opportunity hence relative social equality, and that which made all these possible—republican government."[9]

The novel principles of territorial evolution reached in the Northwest Ordinance included also an ancient technique, the reward of land for military veterans. Congress reserved for Revolutionary War veterans one-seventh (ca. 2,660,000 acres) of the enormous acreage the ordinance embraced to be drawn for by lotteries. Roman and Chinese rulers of antiquity used frontier lands to reward former soldiers and to attract recruits to explore frontiers, with Hadrian's Wall and the Great Wall as examples. More recently, Britain rewarded the United Empire Loyalists in Canada and the anti-Boer military veterans in South Africa with land grants. Japan and Russia granted lands to members of the military units that, respectively, conquered Hakkaido and built the Trans-Siberian railroad. Brazil at present awards lands to troops after service along the Amazon River. All these and other land-grant policies separated military veterans from the mass of a society's citizenry, and rewarded for particular public services a special segment of the public which, like Ulysses returning home war-weary but victorious, it was wise to placate.

In America of the 1780s, placation of state and Continental veterans was clearly in order. Shay's Rebellion was no idle bogeyman. But a simultaneous assumption existed that American soldiers, once victorious, should not be separated from general citizens. The *Independent Chronicle* in Boston encapsulated the view: "To be soldiers and conquerors is one thing: to excel in the arts of peace is another."[10]

In 1787 Congress stipulated that the remainder of the vast Northwest Territory, after the veterans' lotteries, be open for sale to all comers at a dollar an acre minimum. Many thousands of war veterans sold their claims to speculators who resold these rights of access to third parties. Land speculation, endemic throughout our history, raged during the 1780s. Economic conditions, especially the tightness of capital, plus the excess of land over settlers even at the heights of immigrations, encouraged speculations. Proofs remain unsatisfying, however, for long-axiomatic propositions that speculations resulted in high land prices that shut out genuine settlers, dispersed residences unhealthily, invited wasteful farming methods, and encouraged large holdings. Daniel Feller's significant recent reevaluation concluded that these "arguments rested on agrarian postulates that historians are not required to accept." We are beginning to see that the speculations even had certain constructive results. Among them, it helped to prevent creation of segregated communities and to merge veterans' rights into citizens' rights.[11]

If land distributions generated fierce sectional antagonisms, they also encouraged enduringly confident governmental and marketplace processes. The pathbreaking English economist Thomas Malthus's *Essay on the Principles of Population; or, A View of Its Past and Present Effects on Human Happiness*, published in 1798, was hardly dismal to Washington, Adams, Jefferson, or Monroe. Malthus argued (pp. 190, 194) that America, in part because of the swift and orderly availability of Northwest Ordinance land, was the singular exception to the sad fact that populations tended to expand beyond the food supply, thus ensuring impoverished generations unless wars, famines, and epidemics reduced the eating surplus. Americans' "happiness," Malthus wrote, "depended much less upon their peculiar degree of civilization, than upon the peculiarity of their situation, as new colonies, upon their having a great plenty of fertile uncultivated land."

Summing up similar contemporary data, historian Robert H. Wiebe concluded that "by 1840, millions [of Americans] enjoyed an easy faith in the distinctiveness of their society. The heart of their unique America was its democracy, a term that no longer identified [only] the popular element in the republican balance but now covered all the essentials in American life. . . . [It] beckoned to all white Americans who had at least a modest base of property."[12]

In sum, speculators and all, the 1785 Land Law and the 1787 Northwest Ordinance began a series of distributions that transformed successive Wests into stabilized promised lands. Visions of the West as a nursery of republican virtues over a vast continent whose very boundaries were still unknown in 1787 excited Confederation congressmen in New York City and the framers of the Constitution in Philadelphia. Fee-simple ownership by large numbers of smallholders would transform the frontier, where civilization was at risk, into settlements where morality and laws (including responsibilities to repay debts) would be honored and national cohesion maintained. Publicly supported education, a topic in the 1785 and 1787 statutes, would create literate, free farmers who would staff the governments sketched in the 1787 law. Because settlers derived their titles to land and attendant property from the nation, these unservile land-busters and their children, whose right to education was also a statutory duty of government, would be linked in grateful loyalty to the nation and to the new state they had conceived.[13]

This goal of linkage makes understandable why the Northwest Ordinance implanted commitments to public education in the territorial chrysalis of future states. In planning the republic, most supporters of the Constitution and the ordinance espoused not-yet Federalist "loose construction-internal improvement" doctrines and policies. In addition to advocating roads, turnpikes, canals, and forts, such supporters gave priority to various forms of public education, all aiming to make the frontier quickly interdependent with the dismayingly distant East. Schools, one recent commentator suggested, would foster an "empire of system" to temper Jefferson's "empire of liberty."[14] Therefore the 1787 Ordinance is known for its Article III, on schools: "Religion, morality, and knowledge being necessary to good government and the happiness of mankind, schools and the means of education shall forever be encouraged."

A long history underlay this extraordinary provision. Britain's monarchs and other benefactors occasionally favored church-related educational institutions by establishing endowments, commonly from the firmly anticipatable rents of donated, tenanted lands. Analogous efforts here, however, led to failures. As an example, in 1619 the Crown chartered Henrico College in Virginia with a substantial land grant. But underpopulated Virginia, like almost all British North America, could not generate stable incomes from vacant land. Henrico College died. Colonies soon modified the familiar British practice by dedicating to schools, especially colleges, portions of the incomes from lotteries, license fees, ferry tolls, mill services, and certain taxes. Harvard, Yale (the Collegiate School of Connecticut), and William and Mary benefited from these fiscal adaptations. In the eighteenth century, increasing sectarian controversies resulted in newer colleges, including those known now as Princeton, Pennsylvania, Columbia, Brown, and Dartmouth, supplementing incomes from granted lands and prerogatives with private solicitations.

Concerning the lower "common" grades, the constitutions of several states (Vermont, Pennsylvania, North Carolina) pledged support for elementary schools as well as collegiate "seminaries of learning." The Revolution, by preserving and enhancing the colonies-become-states as the base of American federalism, frustrated proponents of a national university and of a national system of education. Congressmen entertained many proposals for dedicating to what would become state-controlled education the income from the sales or rents of federal lands. Jefferson's 1784 Ordinance did not so provide, however, an omission New England's Thomas Pickering and other critics repair by including in the 1785 Land Ordinance the famous clause reserving the sixteenth lot (one section) of every township for the fiscal maintenance of lower schools in that township, a provision that combined nicely with Article III of the 1787 Ordinance quoted earlier. But they remained more pious preachment than mandate until the contract Congress made with the Reverend Manasseh Cutler on behalf of the Ohio Company.

The contract stipulated support for elementary and collegiate education, requiring that "not more than two complete townships [of good land] to be given perpetually for the purposes of a university, . . . to be applied to the intended objects by the legislature of the state."[15] Thereafter, beginning with Ohio in 1803, every new state that was carved from the public lands received this allowance for education. In 1790 Congress extended the substance of the 1785 and 1787 laws to the Southwest, minus antislavery provisions, of course. With Georgia the first in the nation, some states established state universities from their own resources. Most states preferred to exploit the federal 1785 and 1787 laws and created state universities that were partially land-grant in their financing. As the nation, by purchase, conquest, or treaty, acquired territories that spawned new states, the educational systems in these states developed initially around the availability of federal lands. In 1850, Congress increased the grant to two sections in each township (Oklahoma, New Mexico, and Arizona received four sections). Additionally, each new state, on entering the Union, received a further federal gift of two townships (ca. 46,000 acres) for the "seminary of learning," or university. By 1860 the substance of what Congress had provided in response to needs of the nation and the speculations of the Ohio Company, concerning access to land and education, had also migrated westward. Almost a score of publicly supported school systems, including colleges and universities, had blossomed by then in the new states. Whatever the motives of 1787, this sustained governmental support for education from the grades through college, especially in a manner that respected national, state, and local resources, interests, procedures, prejudices, and pride, was globally unique.[16]

In short, Congress looked westward toward the developable frontier that, as Mary Young noted, "has always served as a metaphor of . . . [the] nation's unique potentialities."[17] Perhaps, therefore, the slower evolution toward statehood in the 1787 law, as compared to Jefferson's statute of 1784, was a matter less of contrary purposes than of the pace anticipated for operations of the 1785 Land Law, especially the educational provisions. Tying the 1784 and 1787 laws together were advanced provisions for *gavelkind*, veterans' land bounties, and publicly supported education, plus the famous antislavery provision of the ordinance, Article VI, a policy that alone makes almost fanciful the perennially popular economic interpretations of the 1787 Constitution and Northwest Ordinance as conservative counter-revolutions. Instead, like the Constitution, the ordinance was a consensus product. Contemporaries' sharp differences concerned how best to expand an empire upon republican principles as well as to encourage privileged individuals to profit financially.[18]

Perhaps best capturing the essence of these linked purposes of the ordinance writers of the middle 1780s, in the 1980s Joyce Oldham Appleby discerned among ideas derived from Britain circulating in the new nation, those concerning the self-determination rights of a corporate body, free men's rights to share in public affairs, and the secure possession of private property. Americans, Appleby argued, accepted this derived and restricted catalog as original concerns for liberty. But they also added not only better accommodations for capitalism in this new social order but also a sense of personal freedom only minimally limited to others' enjoyments of the same large personal freedom. The drafters of the ordinance tried to reshape America as a relatively unhierarchical society in which ordinary individuals enjoyed with other undisadvantaged persons access to what most people then believed were major assets of life.[19]

Critics of these positive views, and of their implications for exceptionalist-consensus positions, have not been idle. Gary Nash noted that the ordinance encouraged republican governments for whites at the expense of whole nonwhite cultures that suffered military subjugation; a development leading to Lawrence Wittner's remark that "American exceptionalism becomes particularly questionable when set against the grim premises of 'realism.'" Robert Hill and Paul Finkelman cautioned that, though tiny in number, Indians and Negroes in the territories and states of the Old Northwest were, if nominally free, substantially unequal. Black codes disguised involuntary servitude in the ostensibly free Northwest Territories long after 1787.[20]

Of these criticisms, Finkelman's are the most telling. Boiled down, they underscore imperfections in this state-centered federal Union. Looking ahead from 1787, Finkelman noted correctly how constitutional doctrines and power relationships of federalism and legal doctrines of comity constrained freedom more than slavery. North and South, individuals' moral repugnance to slavery did indeed face discouragingly high barriers. Antislavery litigants who pleaded the Northwest Ordinance found that the federal courts, including the Supreme Court, were often weak and erratic reeds to use as staffs. Such famous decisions as those in *Strader* (1850) and *Dred Scott* (1857) corroded the ordinance as an antislavery base, at least in terms of implementable political positions flowing from constitutional law. Final solutions for slavery in federal territories came, not from courageous decisions of Jeffersonian and Jacksonian high jurists about the Northwest Ordinance as a kind of constitution, but from decisions Lincoln's generation carried on bayonets to Appomattox.[21]

Yet we know also that antislavery lawyers and jurisprudents perpetuated with impressive tenacity and ingenuity the often-flickering abolitionist impulse because hope for its realization existed not only in the 1787 Constitution but more deeply in the Northwest Ordinance. The libertarian antislavery heritage survived even the accommodationist, misnamed "compromises" of 1820, 1833, 1850, and 1854, *Dred Scott*, and the ultimate sectional blackmail, state secessions in 1860 through 1861. The Northwest Ordinance described the future Union of states as it should be. The ordinance, like the Constitution, was a vision as well as a blueprint for immediate implementation. Consistent, sustained federal monitorship of the antislavery clause in the ordinance was not in the cards of history. The national government had only a sparse capacity to implement any policy except revenue-collection, and that, ultimately, by resorting desperately to military coercion as in the "Whiskey Rebellion."[22] Yet, however flaccidly implemented, the ordinance helped to make the laws of the slaveholding states, Lawrence Friedman concluded, appear to be "something alien," dangerous, diseased, and distorted.[23] This alone was a substantial accomplishment. But more benefits than this were to accrue to America from the ordinance.

These ongoing benefits derive from the fact that numerous connections existed between the Declaration of Independence, the Northwest Ordinance, and the Constitution, especially to its Bill of Rights, as well as to other contemporary creations including the first Judiciary Act. These links were, however unanticipatedly, to extend across decades in a manner to affect the configurations and character of the Thirteenth and Fourteenth Amendments of 1865 and 1868, and still further, to *Brown* v. *Board of Education* in 1954 and thus to our time.

Does the antislavery pledge in the Northwest Ordinance link it to larger contexts of American Revolutionary and early national history, and beyond? Not even to a broader Revolutionary context, insisted historian Jack Rakove. He criticized attempts "to locate the Northwest Ordinance within some larger context of Revolutionary enactments," especially the Declaration of Independence and the Constitution's Bill of Rights. Yet Rakove himself conceded that the Declaration of Independence, clauses in the Constitution, and all versions of the ordinance stressed resident individuals' rights of mobility as basic to free society, a view that was to sustain abolitionist jurisprudents through frustrating decades.[24]

It is always important how we perceive the society that produced the ordinance, and, earlier, the 1776 Declaration of Independence and its author, Thomas Jefferson. As Carl Prince noted recently:

> For a long time everybody knew that Thomas Jefferson cribbed the Declaration of Independence and most of his political thought, when it was not uniquely his own, from John Locke. During the

last decade, however, the Lockean Jefferson has been dismissed, and at least five other Jeffersons have appeared in his place; a Bolingbrokean and English Oppositionist Jefferson (Lance Banning), a Scottish Enlightenment moral-sense Jefferson a la Francis Hutcheson (Gary Wills), a Scottish Enlightenment rationalist Jefferson a la Thomas Reid (Morton White), an anti-modern agrarian expansionist Jefferson (Drew McCoy), a champion of commercialism and capitalism Jefferson (Joyce Appleby) [; . . . and] a radical libertarian-communitarian Jefferson (Richard K. Matthews).[25]

So with the Northwest Ordinance. The 1787 Northwest Ordinance was indeed an element in a broad contemporary Jeffersonian current, with the American Revolution as the most immediate and generalized context.

David Brion Davis, in his intriguing 1983 "counter-factual fantasy," after surveying contemporary England, the Caribbean, and Latin America, mused over paths that history might have taken had Britain suppressed its American rebels. He noted that "it was not an army of liberation that Pitt dispatched to rebellious St. Domingue; nor did the British, when they captured Martinique in 1795, intend to implement the French Convention's recent decree of universal emancipation." Further, "in striking contrast to the Northwest Ordinance of 1787, the British Imperial Act of 1790, intended to encourage [white] immigration to Canada, the Bahamas, and Bermuda, allowed whites freely to import all their Negroes [i.e., slaves], household furniture, utensils of husbandry, or clothing." Without the American victory in the Revolution there would have been "no Northwest Ordinance and no truly 'free soil.' "[26]

And in 1984, in factual not counter-factual terms, Davis reinforced his earlier judgment on the globally innovative quality of the ordinance's antislavery commitment. Until the 1770s, slavery and human progress were seen as compatible. But thereafter the ordinance served as a premier proof of a now self-evident truth, that slavery was an unacceptable and uncivilizing evil.

Limits on slavery like those in the ordinance would, many persons asserted, lead to the demise of the bondage system. Its curtailment and eventual death would ensure human progress everywhere. In America, free labor, cheap or free land, popular education, liberal capitalism, constitutional and legal procedures, and political democracy would hasten abolition and be nourished by its deterioration, Davis wrote.[27]

The burden of these analyses is that the ordinance was, if imperfect, exceptional and perhaps unique. True, relatively few blacks ever resided in ordinance states until the turn of the twentieth century. Nevertheless, the majority of white residents of ordinance states fulfilled the hopes of framers of the Constitution and the ordinance better than most judgments allowed. Politically active Ohioans, Indianans, and Illinoisans, as examples, themselves subsequently enforced the substance of the ordinance when they aided runaway slaves via underground railroads and frustrated repetitive efforts to reintroduce slavery.[28] These same voters, however, also introduced, retained, could not erase, and/or strengthened blatantly racist "black codes" in constitutions and laws of their states, not to speak of community customs.

The ordinance was exceptional also concerning individuals' access to legal remedies. Nathan Dane, in drafting the 1787 Ordinance, aimed to preserve the legal rights of residents and nonresidents as the territories evolved toward statehood. Contract performance and rights of possession were continuing concerns of Dane's generation of legalists.[29] As Mark De Wolfe Howe noted, "The intense interest of nineteenth century jurists [and lawyers] in problems of possession is somewhat mystifying [even] to lawyers of the twentieth century."[30]

In addition to a clause against contract impairment, Dane introduced into the 1787 Northwest Ordinance legal rights and remedies guaranteed in the bills of rights for Massachusetts and other states, a commitment that the descent of property be free from "feudal or monarchical" remnants, a place for the rights of habeas corpus and trial by jury, an inheritance provision more liberal than *gavelkind* since females were permitted to share in a deceased father's property, and a stipulation that territorial judges were to use criminal laws of *some* states until a territory, becoming a state, created its own. All these, plus the Article III commitment to public aid for education and the Article VI prohibition against slavery though coming from the floor of Congress rather than from Dane's committee, received his sponsorship and support.[31]

Access to courts was a step toward these manifold, complex, linked goals. Under authority of Article III of the Constitution, the first Congress enacted the famous 1789 Judiciary Act, its "transcendant achievement" according to Felix Frankfurter and James Landis, and another essential context for evaluating the ordinance.[32] By its terms and those of its successor judiciary statutes, the lower federal courts became forums of primary importance in protecting private interests, especially in civil suits involving litigants of diverse state citizenship. State and local courts had proved to be hostile to "strangers." But the congressmen were not hostile to state interests; congressmen were, and are, states' men, only a few becoming statesmen. They had written into the Judiciary Act a requirement that federal judges, including those in territories, when hearing diversity suits, employ the statutes, rules of procedure, and common law of a forum state, a requirement that explains the hurried forum-shopping of generations of lawyers earning their fees. With respect to territorial criminal prosecutions, Congress specified that each territorial legislature choose the criminal law of *some* state, and that territorial judges apply the chosen state law. In short, for civil and criminal actions, Congress created a national context for living in the federal union, while yet honoring legal standards of states.[33]

Does all this claim too much for American policy-makers of the 1780s? Even modern Congresses, though blessed with sophisticated staffs, librarians, and computers, function quickly, vigorously, and imaginatively primarily in crises. Emergencies were common in the 1780s and endemic through 1860. But the systematic application of the laws of the 1780s suggests more than spasmodic reaction to emergencies. By selling ordinance land, Congress was raising revenue, encouraging settlement, discouraging the expansion of slavery, and developing a chain of educational institutions from beginning grades through the collegiate—a sophisticated mix of goals. At the most, as Allen Nevins asserted in 1962, "This vision of rising Western empires, leaning on ever stronger Eastern commonwealths, was pervaded . . . by an assured concept of democracy. Its cornerstone was Jeffersonian equality, the right of every person to an equitable chance in the world, . . . and his fair station before the law." At the least, as Robert H. Wiebe suggested in 1985, formulas developed by all interests in the 1784–87 years "invested the revolutionary republic with a vague, serpentine expandibility."[34] This serpentine expandability, or, better, adaptability and adequacy, was to be the context of major party and courtroom battles of the Ages of Jefferson, Jackson, Lincoln, and Franklin Roosevelt.

As the nineteenth century advanced toward its vital center, evolving concepts of economic and political democracy and of free and unfree labor became defined by individuals' access to degrees of interest in land, whether ownership, leasehold, or other forms. Successive tinkerings with land distribution techniques fanned fierce sectional antagonisms and, at least in the free states, an enduring vision of a confident process and a moral vision of what came to be called social mobility.[35]

By the time the Age of Jackson merged into that of Lincoln, Americans boasted with good reason that, better than any other, their nation knew how to transform subservient territories into equal states, to harmonize individuals' mobility over vast distances with social integration and legal responsibilities, to preserve state-centered, localistically defined, politically stable federalism, and yet allow for measured progress. But America possessed another singular element: the unique presence of millions of blacks living in physical propinquity with white majorities who controlled all levels of government, especially those that counted most, the states and localities. The historic statutes of the 1780s on access to land, education, and legal remedies could not solve the slave law dilemma faced by American democracy and federalism.[36] Only a war—the longest, bloodiest, most searching conflict fought anywhere in the Western world between Napoleon's final defeat and World War I—"solved" that corroding question.

Chapter 2

The 1862 Homestead and Morrill Acts

The very fact that a nation caught up in such a trauma as our Civil War should trouble to legislate on the greater access of its citizens to land, education, and legal remedies is itself singular. Congressmen, creating the 1862 Morrill and Homestead Acts (on education and land), and the 1863 Habeas Corpus Act (on legal remedies), frequently acknowledged the antecedents of these legislations to be in the Declaration of Independence, the Northwest Ordinance, the Bill of Rights, and the first Judiciary Act.[1]

First, a brief look at these remarkable Civil War statutes, beginning with the May 1862 Homestead Act. It afforded loyal adult citizens access to a quarter section of public lands at a minimum $1.25 per acre, with protection for preemptive squatters. Congress gave only a weak priority in homesteading to Union military veterans, one reflecting the aforementioned article of republican faith not to separate soldiers from the mass of citizens. This assumption helps to explain also two globally unique phenomena destined to be carried on in the declared and undeclared wars of the twentieth century. The first phenomenon is the fact that from Sumter to Appomattox, Union states carried on calendared elections including those for humblest sheriffs and justices of the peace to congressmen and presidents. The second is that in the majority of these states, including the most populous, soldiers voted. In Lincoln's memorable phrase, bluecoats were "thinking bayonets"—voting citizens, in short.

The July 1862 Morrill Land-Grant Act granted to loyal states (Congress added the crumpled Confederate states in 1866) an empire (finally, thirteen million acres) of federal land, substantial portions of which each recipient state was to transform into perpetually inviolable endowments for "the support . . . of at least one college where the leading object shall be, without excluding other subjects, scientific and classical studies, and including military tactics, . . . agriculture and mechanic arts, in such manner as the legislatures of the State may respectively prescribe, in order to promote the liberal and practical education of the industrial classes in the several pursuits and professions in life." This was the first nation in the world, whether in peace or war, systematically to commit its resources for the support of higher education, and the Morrill Act scale far transcended even the pioneer Northwest Ordinance. The Morrill Act ensured (i.e., *if* a Union survived the war) local (i.e., state) not national control of derivative collegiate institutions, yet tried to precommit the beneficiary states to make their universities serve the contemporary needs of a swiftly changing society. The lawmakers imposed no restrictions on the gender, religion, or race of students. The statute spoke to the growing popular appreciation of what Charles Beard described in 1937 as *The Unique Function of Education in American Democracy*. Beard's use of the word *unique* deserves emphasis.[2]

Last of the trio, the March 3, 1863, Habeas Corpus Act, plus several amendments from 1866 to 1875, significantly enlarged the jurisdiction of federal courts in certain appeals from allegedly prejudiced state courts, even when diverse state residence, the primary basis of federal jurisdiction since 1789, was not involved.[3] Congress stipulated, additionally, that in appeals, the statutes, legal procedures, and common laws of the forum states must apply, with two exceptions. Negroes' testimony was admissable even adversely to whites, and court officers, lawyers, and jurors must swear to their Union allegiance.[4]

Rooted in the Declaration of Independence, Northwest Ordinance, and first Judiciary Act, these three laws were destined to shape the Thirteenth and Fourteenth Amendments and the Civil Rights Act of 1865–66, which link in turn to momentous public policies of the twentieth century's vital center, especially to the landmark 1954 *Brown v. Board of Education* school desegregation decision of the Supreme Court. Since *Brown,* critics, even those friendly to desegregation, have denied the significance or even the existence of this linkage. Lawyer-writers especially suggest that evidence on school integration from 1866, the year Congress wrote the Fourteenth Amendment, leaves uncertain the intentions and perceptions of its framers. In effect, therefore, the argument runs, in 1954 the justices struck down school segregation on morally justifiable yet largely nonhistorical grounds.[5]

Perhaps brieflike analyses that use history noncontextually, on the alleged weakness of the *Brown* decision, themselves want reconsideration. Although some of my best friends, and one of my children and her husband, are lawyers, the opinion of that usually soft-spoken Princeton historian and former law school associate dean, Stanley Katz, is relevant: "Lawyers are arrogant and think they can do anything, including write [legal] history."[6]

Rarely do law writers on *Brown* recognize the dynamic, mobile, "can do" quality permeating constitutional and legal thought on race and access in the 1860s, or the fact that reformist Republicans, including leaders of the bar Montgomery Blair, Salmon Portland Chase, Thomas McIntyre Cooley, David Dudley Field, Reverdy Johnson, George Washington Paschal, Edwin M. Stanton, William Whiting, and, of course, Abraham Lincoln, acquiesced to "perpetual" slavery in 1860–61. Coerced by state secessions, Republican congressmen, with Lincoln's unhappy assent, wrote and sent out to the states for ratification an "unamendable" Thirteenth Amendment that would bar the nation from ever interfering with slavery in the extant states. Three states ratified this ultimate denial of access before the events of the Civil War made the matter moot.[7]

But thereafter the Union's leaders and, ultimately, voters ascended to advocacy of military emancipation affecting only the occupied Confederacy, then to Congress's nonracial exclusionary provisions for state universities, individuals' homesteads, and legal remedies in 1862–63, then to the national unqualified "freeitude" of the Thirteenth Amendment in 1865. The presence, pace, and force of such changes in our history do not mesh neatly with conclusions that in 1866–68 Lincoln's Republicans rather casually accepted segregation in major policies including the Fourteenth Amendment, and that the 1954 *Brown* decision is thereby suspect.[8]

Legal history has come a long way since *Brown*, a time when eminent Yale law professor Grant Gilmore proclaimed that "there is absolutely no point in setting up a separate category of legal writing (or law teaching) to be known as 'legal history.' "[9] The extent of its growth is measurable in part by the sheer bulk of scholars' commitment to or perceptions about the field (granting that legal history is a field) as represented by relevant professional papers, learned journal articles, and scholarly books. One bibliographer of 1975 needed only a slim volume of 106 pages to list roughly one thousand titles. But, in 1984, another compiler required five fat volumes, listing more than sixty-eight thousand items, to list and cross-list significant titles adequately. The difference reflects not only the bibliographers' differing horizons or even the explosion of interest in the field. It reflects also the fact that many scholars who deal with legal history assume now that it is interlinked with constitutional history and that still-wider linkages tie this combination field to social-cultural contexts that illuminate the subtly woven fabrics of technical law and constitutional change.[10]

This assumption about context and linkages evidences itself also in almost every subfield of history. Recent histories of education, as an example, argue for every researcher more seriously to accommodate community as a mix of dynamic contextual issues.[11] Historians of wars and battles, elections, cities, science, and business share this concern. Scholarly debates on the significance of, as examples, social mobility in the Age of Jackson or blacks' immobility in Reconstruction labor markets are most useful when contextually considered.[12]

As with any approach to history, this emphasis on context has hazards. Some "new" historians so stress mass contextual data as to worry Thomas Bender, who wrote that "to the extent that these ever deeper explorations into the interiors of subcultures succeed, one is more and more confronted with the irreducible particularity that obscures the common and relational elements that make an American history." And Harry Scheiber of Berkeley warned that "the new legal history manages to push landmarks like federalism or the Civil War into the background."[13]

Neither federalism nor the Civil War deserve to fade into irrelevance.[14] Middle grounds exist between monocular focus on black letter, "positive" law and "macro" views of the "blinding lights" of history.[15] These middle grounds offer comfort to those disturbed by the implicit position of the Warren Court in *Brown*, that history from the 1860s has little if any illumination for 1954, a position that delights anti-*Brown* crusaders of 1985. Instead, evidence from this middle ground suggests, as noted earlier, that the *Brown* decision was justifiable not "only" because of the immorality of segregation but also because it rested on sounder history than the Warren Court knew.

The evidence derives in part from the Homestead, Morrill, and Habeas Corpus Acts of 1862–63, considered in the contexts of the Thirteenth Amendment of 1865 and their antecedents, the Northwest Ordinance, the Declaration of Independence, and the Bill of Rights. Taken together, the progression of these policies suggests that the Civil War and Reconstruction pushed white America toward goals transcending reunion. It suggests also that during the 1860s access to the most treasured fruits of American life increased substantially for most whites and many blacks, these benefits including access to land, education, and legal remedies. Further still, this evidence indicates the Lincoln administration adapted to unanticipatable situations a heritage, wrote historian Donald Pickens, "of [John Locke's and] Scottish common sense philosophy, Adam Smith's *laissez-faire* creed, and Puritan religious sentiments. In addition, this [new Republican] synthesis provided the basis for . . . understanding the transformation of the American War of Independence . . . from 1776 to 1865 and beyond."[16]

Fortunately the idea of connectives between 1776 and 1865, between the Declaration of Independence and the Thirteenth and Fourteenth Amendments, no longer startles many historians, and important law writers are contributing to this healthy research tide.[17] That tide takes us to contextual aspects of the Fourteenth Amendment relevant to *Brown*.

An informative—no, essential—context for the Fourteenth Amendment and therefore for *Brown* remains the too-long-overlooked trio of access laws of 1862–63, considered by contemporaries as essential sources as well as definitions of the Thirteenth Amendment of 1865 and the Fourteenth Amendment of 1866. Stated another way, the Thirteenth and Fourteenth Amendments were born not only out of the Civil War itself, but also from efforts extending back thirty years of abolitionist lawyers, including Salmon Chase, Charles Sumner, and William Whiting, to return public policies to the principles of the Declaration of Independence and the Northwest Ordinance.[18] With the Civil War, the small minority of antislavery champions successfully linked their eventually great cause with patriotic nationalism and also with continued respect for the state-based federal system as the only acceptable foundation for private rights.[19] This linkage among state rights nationalists raised the question: if abolition ever occurred, how could the woefully underinstitutionalized American government shield the millions of freedmen?

During the pre-1860 decades when young, upwardly mobile lawyer Lincoln was climbing professional and political ladders, government, especially the national government, encouraged, but itself rarely implemented, public work. Alexis de Tocqueville reported accurately that "the citizen of the United States is taught from infancy to rely upon his own exertions in order to resist the evils and the difficulties of life."[20] This habit links the eighteenth-century "republican [small 'r'] synthesis" with that which Lincoln's Republicans (capital "R") perceived, pursued, and, partially at least, achieved in the heat of the Civil War and Reconstruction. The new Republican synthesis retained a self-help emphasis and augmented essentially noncoercive roles for government on all levels of the federal system.[21]

By 1865 in Union states, this refined Republican synthesis exhibited itself in relatively color-blind (though rarely gender-blind) extensions of suffrage and legal remedies as basic to self-help and self-protections. Voting majorities of states, themselves enlarging by reason of wartime reforms in state constitutions, accepted the Republican marriage of adequacy constitutionalism and novel uses for public law. Voting and litigating allowed individuals to protect their access to the enhanced categories of public services that the new era was calling into existence: schools, asylums, police, urban utilities, streetcars, firefighters, and orphanages among others. The admission and exclusion of blacks, white women, and former rebel whites from these enhanced services, from licensed callings, and from elective or appointed offices became first political, then legal and constitutional issues on local, then state, then Washington stages. Republicans, rejecting state sovereignty constitutional dogmas, hailed Massachusetts Chief Judge Lemuel Shaw's newer "state police power" doctrine. Columbia Professor Francis Lieber, celebrating the news of Appomattox, paid tribute to the bluecoats who had won nationhood. But by nation, Lieber added, "I do not mean centralization."[22]

The Republicans' mixtures of agrarian values with Federalist-Whig constitutional and legal doctrines encouraged changes. These often-uncomfortable changes allowed Democrats to disassociate from secession and treason and, in political campaigns and courtroom procedures, to champion static state rights and white-only rights. Lincoln came to accept basic assumptions of abolitionist jurisprudents: that democratic federalism was evolutionary not static, that the Constitution was adequate to all unfolding needs including emancipation and race equality, and that the war powers of the nation (i.e., both of the President and Congress) could extend even into states.[23] In short, the Republicans' wartime synthesis included the Declaration of Independence, federalism, constitutionalism, and acquisitive individualism leading to economic and social mobility, all reflected in the Homestead, Morrill, and Habeas Corpus laws.

As suggested earlier, supporters of the Thirteenth Amendment often defined it in terms of these laws and their antecedents. Individuals' equality in the lawyers' trinity of rights—remedies and responsibilities before all levels of law and authority in the multilayered federal system—was the keystone for the wartime Republican arch. In the 1862 and 1863 laws on access, Republicans, clinging to this trinity and to the self-help ethic Tocqueville perceived, espoused public policies designed to make self-help more realistic and meaningful. Although responding to urgent immediate needs, these policies retained state, local, and individual implementation. Settlers themselves triggered the procedures of the Homestead and Morrill Acts; plaintiffs enforced their enlarged rights in federal courts that the Habeas Corpus Act made available, as well as in state courts. Although federal capacities for monitoring states or individuals remained underwhelmingly thin throughout the decade—a fact that boded ill for effective implementation of the civil rights laws of the late 1860s and early 1870s—land offices and courts were familiar, comfortable, and unthreatening institutions. Thinly staffed, inexpensive, and uncoercive, save to losers in litigations, with few and brief exceptions these institutions became quickly and generally available to former greybacks as well as to former bluecoats.[24]

Disagreeing, historians Harry Scheiber and William Miller argue impressively that centralization did occur, especially in "national" banking and federal tax collecting.[25] No doubt the Union victory altered historic diffusions of power. But in the context of penalties that losers in civil wars suffered abroad in the mid-nineteenth century (not to speak of the late twentieth) can greater vigor by federal revenue agents equal centralization? Postwar federally chartered banks under the 1863 National Banking Act neither obliterated nor controlled state-chartered private banks, nor, as the sponsor of the bill, Ohio Senator John Sherman noted in 1863, were these the purposes of the law. The drastic oscillations in money markets between the 1863 banking act of Lincoln's administration and the Federal Reserve Act of Wilson's hardly reflect centralization.[26]

Instead, after Appomattox as never before Sumter, American states became what one English lawyer described as the "great transatlantic workshop" where Britishers should look for "Yankee notions" as "models in working order of all our projected reforms." He noted admiringly that "the United States are generally the *vile corpus* out of which by dint of many an experiment, essay, and strange vagary, the good comes by which we tardily profit. The American loves to dabble in those subjects which are somewhat vaguely known as 'Social Science,' and we believe that in State or another in the Union . . . education, crime, legal reforms, sanitary improvements, and so on, has been further sifted than at home. . . . A little more attention to Yankee notions would not be thrown away."[27]

"Yankee notions," products of the Republicans' permissive, evolutionary, "can do" constitutionalism, to which they added an elastic war powers gloss, permitted party spokesmen from Lincoln down to perceive of the war as revolution and as constitutional conservator. Peyton McCrary concluded recently that "by accepting the moral legitimacy of revolution, they were also able to take more seriously the radical implications of their own Declaration of Independence. The principles of 1776 had long been a centerpiece of the Republican ideology, . . . but only the war made possible the extension of the idea that 'all men are created equal' to include the Afro-American population."[28]

This inclusion developed logically from "freedom national" ideas of the aforementioned abolitionist lawyers, ideas long antedating the Civil War. A generation of Republican voters, including Lincoln and ballot-casting white and black bluecoats, concluded that heritages of the American Revolution, including the Declaration of Independence, the Constitution, and the Northwest Ordinance, were what the Civil War was about. The embattled Union must encourage the states—all the states—to afford a state resident formal equality before the laws of his state as the primary definition of nationwide republican government.[29]

The Thirteenth Amendment embraced this vision. Its adherents were of course conscious of tenacious racism in northern states, commonly including "black code" segregations and Jim Crow exclusions from streetcars, schools, and balloting, antimiscegenation policies and unpunished racial violence.[30] Nevertheless, the Thirteenth Amendment seemed finally to harmonize the new Republican synthesis with the fact that states and localities defined almost all legal rights, remedies, and responsibilities in individuals' economic relationships (civil rights), in criminal justice, and in what we now label civil liberties. The Thirteenth Amendment made individuals free and equal where it counted, in their community and state as well as nationally. It restrained not only nation and states but all officials and private individuals from acting or failing to act in ways that reduced other persons to involuntary servitude, a condition that only the future contexts of particular situations would define (which explains why Congress appended an enforcement clause, the first in the Constitution for an amendment). By prohibiting involuntary servitude everywhere, the amendment imposed a positive duty on all authorities and private persons to sustain freedom, a position sustained in 1866 and 1867 by Chief Justice Chase and Justice Noah Swayne, on circuits.[31]

In prewar America, freedom was primarily the undefined condition of whites, and, in the free states, of blacks as well, a condition achieved by birth. In 1865 Republicans were optimistic about avoiding coercive government initiatives in the novel arena of implementing freedom defined as equality, in part because the 1862 Homestead and Morrill Acts and the 1863 Habeas Corpus Act had already enlarged access to the best self-protections for freedom and equality that the generation knew: land, education, and litigations. No one in 1865 predicted a need for more amendments, much less *the* Fourteenth or Fifteenth Amendments or military reconstruction laws, plus their batteries of coercive implementing statutes.

The Republican synthesis of 1865, as illustrated by the Thirteenth Amendment, was extraordinarily open in potentialities. Lincoln's own wartime evolution toward radical Republican positions on race, and, along with his party majority, to policies favoring equal access to education, land, and legal remedies, connected the liberal past to immediate needs and to enlarged auguries for the future. As is well known, Lincoln, though always unsympathetic to slavery, was no abolitionist activist when he became president. But as the Civil War progressed this educable man dropped his earlier advocacy of colonization abroad for free slaves, a process aiming at whiteness as a definition for free soil. Instead by 1865 he accepted a vision of a slaveless, biracial America in which millions of both races would coexist in physical legal propinquity on terms of legal equality defined, as for whites, by their states and communities.

In 1865, the year of the Thirteenth Amendment, the question of blacks' access to public education became a war aim—one unthinkable in 1861 and only timidly advanceable even in late 1863 or 1864. Lincoln, in his December 8, 1863, war powers proclamation on state reconstructions, pardons, and amnesty, promised to support "any provision" by a returning state that declared "permanent freedom" for all its Negro citizens (i.e., residents) "and provided for their education." In 1864 he secretly suggested to the Union military governor of Louisiana that former black bluecoats vote there, but he did not press the exceedingly delicate matter.[32] Then, with a second term won that would keep him in office until March 1869, and with the proposed Thirteenth Amendment out to the states for ratification, in an April 11, 1865, public address Lincoln redefined postvictory Reconstruction, a process dependent until then on the uncertain base of a president's war powers, in terms of the more permanent form of a constitutional amendment. He would use his carryover commander-in-chief and war powers under the soon-to-be-amended Constitution, Lincoln stated, publicly this time, to encourage the crumpled Confederate states to allow literate blacks, especially Negro veterans of Union armies, to vote and to accept in public schools children of both races, the latter without commitment to segregation or integration. No less an authority than John Wilkes Booth, on hearing this speech, equated it with "nigger citizenship."[33]

Lincoln had defined the viable postwar agenda of the antislavery generation in his open ascent into radical Republican ranks. He had never identified himself publicly with any policy until he was ready to pursue it, and of course had no foreknowledge that Booth and his fellow conspirators had determined on political murder, one that must be accounted as one of the most successful in history. Lincoln's successor, Andrew Johnson, had sharply differing and ineducable views on desirable federal policy on race equality in education or anything else. By 1868, when state voters ratified the Fourteenth Amendment, Johnson, despite the impeachment, had already blunted the precarious commitment to effective enforcement of biracial equality of access. To be sure, his obstructionism also inspired the creation and ratification of the Fourteenth Amendment, which, if divorced from the context of the Thirteenth Amendment, as it has been, limits only official state action.[34]

Can our contemporaries equally successfully blunt these historical though recently rerecognized commitments to race and gender equality? Assumptions concerning *Brown* v. *Board of Education* and the 1866 and 1965 civil rights laws analogous to those Andrew Johnson possessed, as noted earlier, appear to be popular again in Washington. These misreadings of history encourage efforts to reverse equalitarian policies spinning off from the "burden of *Brown*." Therefore stress is justified on the burdens—and inspirations—of history that the creators and ratifiers of the Thirteenth Amendment bore with them to Appomattox and beyond.

Models for "beyond" were the 1862–63 federal laws on access. Consider education as a public duty. Northern state voters were so convinced about the benefits of public education that they interfered by statutes even with family relationships, in the form of required attendance-truant officer coercions, and raised property taxes to finance public school systems. Sophisticated not primitive in their concerns about education, the Lincoln Republicans accepted the judgments of professionalizing educators that illiteracy, slavery, secession, and disloyalty were cancers capable of destroying not only the Union of states but all states, Northern and Southern, all property and all morality. So pervasive was this climate of opinion, remarked John Y. Simon, a close student of the 1862 Land Grant–College Bill, that "one need not ask how [Congressman Justin Smith] Morrill got the idea for his bill, but how he could have avoided it."[35] Despite opposition by President Johnson and by whites in Southern states to which Congress beginning in 1866 extended the essence of the Morrill and Homestead Acts, Congress had established ties between access to homesteads and support for higher public education for blacks.[36]

Times changed. By 1890 Justin Morrill still championed federal supports for state-run higher education, especially land grants. But he had also become a nonopponent to racial segregation in education. Law Professor Avins took Morrill's career to be a proof of a proposition that "the Fourteenth Amendment does not cover education at all, or give the federal courts the power to control state policies in regard to higher education, whether those policies relate to racial segregation or otherwise."[37]

Alternative conclusions are viable. Viewed in its dynamic contemporary context, policies embraced in the years from the Morrill Act to the Thirteenth Amendment suggest a brave if fragile outreaching toward new frontiers of color-blind equality of access. Even in 1865, the year of ratification of the Thirteenth Amendment, Frederick Douglass worried to Lydia M. Child that "unfriendly legislation by a state may undo all the friendly legislation by the Federal Government." Three years later, in 1868, the year of ratification of the Fourteenth Amendment and of Johnson's impeachment, abolitionist jurisprudent J. C. Hurd and Republican constitutionalist Lieber agreed that "just now it looks as if the question of state rights in our national politics were about to make new trouble."[38] This was also the year that Thomas McIntyre Cooley published what was to become the first of many editions of his *Constitutional Limitations,* a book that was destined to serve generations of paper-chasing students in Langdellian law schools soon to be born. Georgia Republican

Amos T. Akerman, soon (1870) to be Grant's attorney general, advised Massachusetts Senator Charles Sumner that because the Civil War had made the constitutional system "more national [only] in theory," even Republican stalwarts like Morrill expressed "a hesitation to exercise the powers to redress wrongs in the states."[39]

The Supreme Court was part of the cause of the hesitation. By 1866 its astonishing, still inadequately explored revival from the *Dred Scott* depths of 1857 was under way. It had signaled its climb in the 1862 *Prize Cases* when, by a single vote, the justices sustained the legitimacy of a war already two years old. Then, in the far more alpine outreach of the 1867 *Test Oath* decisions, the jurists, by five to four, declared against the constitutionality not only of a federal law but of a state constitution. Only a few years later, in the 1873 *Slaughterhouse* decision, the Supreme Court held that the defendable federal rights of national citizenship were few and insignificant, inventing the tradition that the Fourteenth Amendment limited itself to federal and state public (i.e., "positive") laws, and did not affect nonactions by officials or the host of community customs and private actions capable then and since of reducing individuals to "involuntary servitude." *Slaughterhouse* and its unillustrious progeny to *Plessy* v. *Ferguson* helped to make respectable states' denials of blacks' access to federally subsidized land-grant and state universities, to homesteads, or to federal courts, and the access of white women to licensed professions.

So defined, the Fourteenth Amendment quickly overshadowed the far vaster implications of the Thirteenth Amendment and made it seem that the emancipation amendment, if not repealed by the Fourteenth, was a finished, superfluous appendage to the Constitution once states ceased formally defining humans as property.[40] In short, *Slaughterhouse*, followed soon by *Cruikshank, Granger,* and that familiar string leading to *Plessy* at the turn of this century, substantially redirected the nature of

the contextual "package" of the Thirteenth and Fourteenth
Amendments away from the potentially universal and integra-
tionist visions of 1865 and 1866.[41]

Reconstruction "ended" and Americans celebrated the
centennial of their Revolution in 1876, the year when a brand
new Heidelberg Ph.D. and history fellow of the equally new
Johns Hopkins University reached Baltimore. In his Hopkins
seminars, young Herbert Baxter Adams advanced an evolutionary "germ theory" of national development derived from his
Heidelberg mentors, a theory in which American constitutional
forms and democratic practices grew from Teutonic and Anglo-
Saxon "racial" seeds. A shrewd academic gamesman as well as
able scholar, Adams cultivated regional social and business elites. His special lectures stressed the leadership of Maryland in
assigning western land claims to the national government in the
1780s. Proud Marylanders applauded Adams's assertion that the
resulting expanded material interests were more important than
the creation of the Articles of Confederation or the Constitution.
There could, he iterated, be "no state [i.e., nation] without a
people, no state without land: these are the fundamental principles of political science and were recognized as early as the days
of Aristotle."[42]

Wisconsinian Frederick Jackson Turner joined Adams's semi-
nar in the late 1880s, just when the federal government opened
the Oklahoma territory to homesteading in a spectacular "land
rush" of would-be agricultural entrepreneurs. Turner, un-
satisfied by his mentor's germ theory, developed more "scientific" approaches that, according to one analyst, provided "a historical summit from which to view American history."
Descending from this summit in 1893, Turner unveiled his
"frontier thesis," developing it subsequently in a thin body of
vastly influential papers and publications. He encapsulated his
environmentalist argument: "The existence of an area of free

land, its continuous recession, and the advance of American settlement westward, explain American development." On this land settlers threw off European chains of class and hierarchy, moved upward in status and material possessions, and participated in political democracy and economic opportunity, thus forming the American character and peculiarly American institutions. The end of free or cheap land must lead to social homogeneity and a lessening of individualism, democracy, social mobility, and opportunity.[43]

Turner's evaluations, and, in the ensuing three quarters of a century, those in the pride of his students and intellectual beneficiaries, unleashed a large, rich, and often-acrimonious literature about Turnerian concepts. Some critics discredited Turner because he too uncritically asserted the benefits of American life, especially those provided by unequaled opportunity to own or rent land. As an example, David Potter asserted that "Turner did not recognize that the attraction of the frontier was simply as the most accessible form of abundance, and therefore he could not conceive that other forms of abundance might replace it as the lodestone to which the needle of American aspirations would point."[44]

If Turner could not conceive of what Potter called "other forms of abundance," others could. Charles Beard, one of the most illustrious and influential of Turner's critics, conceived of the singular commitment by urban and rural taxpaying voters to public education as the most important alternative "form of abundance." Despite his reputation as an iconoclastic muckraker, Beard, in his 1937 monograph entitled *The Unique Function of Education in American Democracy*, suggested that "the association of educational history with the encompassing history of American civilization is not a form of antiquarianism and dust-sifting. On the contrary by this process alone does it seem possible to obtain sure guidance in the formulation of an educational policy corresponding to the realities of the living present, now rising out of the past." So viewed, Beard continued, the Civil War was indeed a second American Revolution, but one by no means of predominantly selfish, mean-spirited characteristics. Instead, the policies of increased access to education and other fruits of American life generated during the Civil War and Reconstruction preserved and democratized the nation, widened liberty by establishing equality of access as the duty of society, and profoundly stimulated individual enterprise because "education equalized opportunity for training."[45]

Many analysts have since denied the significance of what Beard discerned. They stressed instead the frequent, bitter party battles of Gilded Age–New Deal decades, including those concerning implementations and adaptations of the Homestead and Morrill Acts. Noting how Congresses, responding to special interests, modified the Homestead law to favor cattle barons and exploiters of mineral, timber, and water resources, historians described land grabs since the Revolutionary and Mexican wars when nation and states gave military veterans land scrip, much of which passed to speculators. Scholars stressed the favoritism to the populous eastern states implicit in a formula that tied land allotments to a state to a ratio of thirty thousand acres of federal land for each representative and senator, and at exposés of venal officials of states selling Homestead and Morrill Act scrip at foolishly low prices, so depriving their infant universities of potentially larger incomes. Historians concluded also that reform attempts from 1862 to 1935 were disappointing. Homesteads remained alienable, and the statute's safeguards against speculators proved to be inadequate. Congresses, without meaningful controls over resales, speculations, and monopolies, dedicated enormous acreage to railroads and other "internal improvements," and almost 500 million acres to states and territories, while exempting these grants from free land approaches of the Homestead law. Thus a dual land system developed, one of special congressional grants and the other, often involving inferior lands, deriving from the Homestead Act. Yet, after developing this powerful catalog of misdeeds and misdirected opportunities, Paul Gates concluded that the Homestead Act and its amendments possessed "noble purpose" and played a "great part . . . in enabling nearly a million and a half people to acquire farm land, much of which they developed into farm homes, [and these results] far outweigh the misuse to which they were put."[46]

Recent interpretations stress anachronisms involved in judging nineteenth-century standards of public administration by higher minima. Save theoretically, no pre–New Deal Congress could have deleted these unsavory features from the 1862 laws or grant money directly to higher education (except to Gallaudet College for the blind, to Howard University for blacks, both in the federal district, to the military academies, and to Indian schools on federal reservations). The interests of the nation in swift development of its territories took precedence over fiduciary responsibility.[47]

Parallel limitations on adequate federal monitorship existed in education. Save for thin reporting responsibilities, state beneficiaries of the Morrill Act, though developing public education into their fourth branch of government, were virtually (though not virtuously) free of federal reins. Critics, including presidents of competing private and state colleges, emphasized inadequate laboratories and skeletal library holdings at land-grant institutions, without mentioning that many private and nonland-grant state universities were also ill-equipped. Congress's stress on technical jobs for the future colleges ultimately redirected whole sciences and professions and raised educational standards at all levels.[48]

Ultimately is a big word. Concerning research and teaching, for a long time even the best land-grant institutions had low reputations even among well-wishers, and state university and Ivy League critics thought them laughable. In their first fifty years, according to one critic, "The best [land-grant school] called for apology; the worst [were] . . . appalling." Carpers mocked the anemic student enrollments at the "cow colleges," which served mere corporals' guards at a time when homesteading embraced hundreds of thousands. In many states, elementary and secondary school systems produced sparse matriculants for the new colleges. The University of Wisconsin long retained the name and function of "High School for the Village of Madison," and Pennsylvania State University was the "Farmers' High School." Total student enrollments of sixty to four hundred were common for decades at California and Kansas.[49]

Yet similar low numbers obtained also at Harvard where only 637 students enrolled in 1872, Princeton half that, Columbia 124, and 88 at Pennsylvania. In the 1880s (as in the 1980s), deficiencies in elementary and secondary schools forced land-grant universities into essentially remedial functions in part because some constitutions of states, as in Indiana, Illinois, and Texas, well into the twentieth century required their universities to admit all secondary school graduates.

As if to balance this deleterious catalog, Morrill Act universities, Abraham Flexner perceived in 1910, were also escalating standards of the secondary school and teacher-training systems in their states. Both effects, indeed, though paradoxical were occurring simultaneously and intermixing in subtle and complex ways.[50] By World War I, the Morrill Act institutions as well as the older state universities were allocating increasing shares of their resources for the enhanced research libraries and laboratories and faculty talent essential for the new theoretical and applied sciences (including the social sciences). Resulting stirs in the academic disciplines and professions also shook the historic undergraduate liberal arts colleges, whether secular or church-related, evoking difficult questions about the traditional character-building emphases of these institutions.

Old, still frankly elitist Ivy League universities and new, equally picky graduate- and science-focused institutions, including Hopkins, Chicago, and Stanford, seemed by their very histories and styles, not to mention resources, to outshine the relatively democratized Morrill Act schools. But beneath postures of austere, confident superiority, by the 1890s all universities were caught up in reassessments and explosions of knowledge. Academics, as an example, though in the main delighted by the accelerated access to research data that the new card catalogs provided, were unsure how to keep pedagogy abreast of the fallout. All universities were competing for frontrunning faculty, superior students, increased endowments, and general prestige. A national academics' profession, as distinguished from licensed teachers' professional associations, was coming into being, one marked by loyalties more to disciplines than to employing institutions.

Some of the derision heaped on the "ag" and "cow" colleges in their early decades requires skeptical evaluation in light of these factors. The ongoing commitments of the Morrill Act schools to unprestigious (in critics' views) applied fields, such as teacher-training, home economics, and farm management, should not have obscured for so long the widening contribution of these same universities to "pure" research and increasingly significant libraries (with that of the University of Illinois one day to rank only below that of Harvard and Yale).[51]

Obscured they were. Aesthetes satirized even the locations of many Morrill Act and state university campuses, whose faculty often eased the critics' task by perpetuating folklore about political deals at state capitals and county courthouses in which a "winning" community got a state insane asylum or penitentiary and the "loser" received the land-grant university as consolation prize. The efforts of state lawmakers and regents to protect undergraduates' physical and perhaps intellectual virginities by locating most land-grant and/or state universities in state capitals and in semirural towns as at Ann Arbor, Athens, Bloomington, Columbia, Columbus, Madison, and Urbana appeared comical along the Charles or Hudson rivers. Or, perhaps, sinister in the opinions of muckraking Progressive-era analysts, since these bucolic locations, perhaps by design, for many decades attracted relatively few urban Catholics, Jews, and blacks. Few cities then supported tuition-free or low-tuition municipal colleges much less universities offering quality graduate and professional degrees. Private institutions, often Catholic church–related, though requiring substantial tuitions, only partially filled urban voids. Thin scholarly evidence and literary insights from John Dos Passos, Meyer Levin, Sinclair Lewis, and George R. Stewart, among others, suggest that the rural locations of land-grant universities, political foot-dragging on substantial urban branches, and discriminatory admissions policies perpetuated serious "upstate-downstate" gulfs. These abysses endured until the 1944 G.I. Bill and the 1954 Supreme Court *Brown* v. *Board of Education* and 1963 *Baker* v. *Carr* "one-man, one-vote" decisions better equalized urbanites' status in state politics and greatly widened their access to public benefits. But this peers too far ahead.

Ascending toward their present eminences, early state and land-grant universities linked with licensed professions and established standards for admission to relevant degree programs and licensed practice. Universities and professional associations commonly contrived means to exclude women and racial/ethnic religious minorities from entry or practice.[52] In sum, avarice and prejudice existed in the administrations of the Homestead and Morrill Acts. But, historian Paul Varg concluded, so did selflessness and loftiness of purpose that "extend[ed] to the sons of farmers and mechanics the richness which life possesses when endowed with the philosophical habit."[53] And a major scholarly critic of the land-grant schools concluded that:

Nothing did more *eventually* for mass or democratized education. . . . They were committed, they opened their doors, and they
pressed fate with action. Their early contribution was the ardent
conviction and the provision of opportunity, the expectation, and
the ideal, not the actual achievement. They were ahead of their
times. . . . When the ideal did blossom, it did so magnificently.[54]

The Morrill Act was formally gender-blind. But the Supreme Court's 1873 *Slaughterhouse* decision broadcast to the legal
and teaching professions the notion that, despite state and
federal bills of rights and the Thirteenth and Fourteenth Amendments, the states could disfavor whole classes of state (and,
therefore, of federal) citizens from access to professional educations newly required for practice. In the same year as *Slaughterhouse*, the justices rejected Myra Bradwell's petition that the
Fourteenth Amendment forbade Illinois from barring her from
the bar despite her fine qualifications for legal practice. Two
years later, in *Minor* v. *Happersett*, the Court ruled that states
could restrict voting to males without violating that amendment. Law writers like Thomas McIntyre Cooley who were com-
posing constitutional commentaries for the new Langdell-style
law schools, many of which were associating with land-grant
universities, further dignified the inventive proposition of the
Court. In short, access to the highest court failed fully to open
professions or suffrage to women.[55]

But some "disorderly women" refused to be stuffed like ge-
nies into that historic bottle, the home. Shouldering into professional degree programs and practice, they helped to preserve
claims on federal and state justice and on fairer shares of state
budgets for schools and other public facilities, while refining relevant legal and constitutional doctrines and developing future
leadership cadres. More than the tiny Seven Sisters, the state
and land-grant universities, Elizabeth Janeway concluded,
"were not only educating mothers- and housewives-to-be, but
offering the company of educated women alternative profes-

sional careers. Intimate alumnae connections developed among those who chose careers over marriage. Old female ties were re-created in long and close friendships, while college campuses or settlement houses substituted for family homes."[56]

Ambitious, determined, and able females wrested B.A.s, LL.B.s, M.A.s, and Ph.D.s from Victorian and Edwardian male administrators and academics who usually blocked their entry into "unwomanly" degree programs, or pressured them into "women's" curricula, especially elementary education, home economics, nursing, and librarianship. So pressured, Louisa Allen Gregory developed an innovative domestic-science program for the Illinois Normal University in the 1870s, of which institution she was an alumna. If only because no one thought to block their entry, INU had allowed women into science courses, and Gregory applied her lab training to the task of creating curricula in better household management.

By contrast, Florence Bascom refused deflection to ladylike pursuits and forced her way into the graduate geology curriculum at the University of Wisconsin and Johns Hopkins, becoming the first woman to receive a Ph.D. from the latter institution. Similarly, in nonscience areas, Texan Oveta Culp Hobby and Nebraskan Mari Sandoz both transcended their families' economic situations (Sandoz emerging from especially hardscrabble rural homestead origins), because their respective state universities afforded them opportunities to parlay opportunities, talents, and tenacity into significant careers. Among the first women admitted even as an auditor to the University of Texas School of Law, Hobby (née Culp), unable to continue without a job, wrangled herself a patronage appointment as the first female parliamentarian of the Texas Senate, a position in which she was a marked success. After marrying the then-governor, Hobby became, successively, a communications tycoon, the first commander of the World War II Women's Army Corps, and the first

Secretary of Health, Education, and Welfare.[57] Sandoz, that fine West-facing author of *Old Jules* (1935) and *Crazy Horse* (1942) among other engaging fiction, and of estimable nonfiction including *The Cattlemen* (1958), was the daughter of a Nebraska homesteader who went busted several times, but, who, persevering, finally created a decent living for his family. Despite deficiencies in her rural education, young Sandoz taught in grade schools until the University of Nebraska admitted her as an "adult special" student. She remained in this limbo from 1922 to 1931, earning pittances as an exam grader and proofreader. Sandoz believed that her subsequent career attested to the opportunity the Morrill Act created for her to learn her craft. And of her father, she wrote, "The Homestead Act was the hope of the poor man."[58]

The struggles of many such intensely motivated women prepared them not only for professional and other careers but also for effective political action. In the coeducational Morrill Act and state universities, North and South, they necessarily learned how to exploit the resources of large, complex, collective institutions. A few themselves ran for state elective office, sometimes winning. They applied their training and insights in political lobbying for antichild labor statutes, settlement house administration, and exposé journalism, so shaping Populism, Progressivism, and the New Deal. Kathryn Kish Sklar, after reevaluating Florence Kelley's career, argued recently that:

> American women played a more important part in the process of the creation of the 'social welfare state' than was the case elsewhere. Two sets of reasons explain their greater power; one had to do with the greater access American women had to social resources such as education, one having to do with the greater demand for their skills in the United States, where in comparison with other industrializing nations, such as Germany and Great Britain, there was a relative political vacuum of male leadership on these 'social welfare' issues.[59]

Race was another matter. Familiar separate-but-unequal evasions of the Fourteenth Amendment by Southern states included segregated land-grant institutions for blacks. By 1887 W. E. B. Du Bois's "Open Letter to the Southern [White] People" conceded that "the vast majority of the Negro race, thanks in great measure to your own lack of foresight, are not intelligent." By World War I, the general effects of segregation, and of discriminatory state funding in particular, were exaggeratedly visible in skewed "scientific" aptitude and IQ tests. Yet generations of striving black youths obtained inexpensive postsecondary educations, many in segregated and unsegregated land-grant schools, and, Du Bois included, became apostles of Americans' secular religion, education. They created enduring heritages of respect for learning and imposed claims on white society for more equal access to its fruits.[60] Even in the deepest Jim Crow decades, probably more American nonwhites received higher educations than was true of blacks in the rest of the world.

That access of blacks to education endured at all in the redeemer South, in segregated institutions of course, is attributable in part to spasmodic federal pressures after 1877, and to the fact that, considering impediments and risks, impressively large clusters of blacks homesteaded under the 1862 law and its amendments. Resulting Negro enclaves of residence sometimes meant black control of balance-of-power electoral situations in close districts and when Republicans controlled national offices if terrorism was suppressed. Such chancy situations occasionally impelled white politicos to appropriate fairer shares of tax money to black land-grant schools, asylums, and other public institutions.[61]

These eclectic developments suggest that the analyst of Tennessee black land-grant colleges was correct to conclude that the Morrill Act "created a legislative mechanism for synthesizing . . . ideas [on multiracial access] into an educational formula of inestimable importance."[62] The numerous idiosyncratic patterns in the access of females and blacks (and, elsewhere, of Indians, Asians, and Hispanics) also reflect the fact that higher education history has always been, and remains, state and local history. This connection between the democratized politics of federalism and the purposes and policies of higher education bred numerous foolishnesses and wrongs. They include commercialized "sports" and almost-dehumanized large class sizes. Red Scare and Accuracy in Academia-style interferences in educational policy by pressure groups and politicians mar the past and tar the present. But this connection also inspired or allowed development of universities' extension and correspondence courses, of the University of Iowa's Writers' Conferences, and of the University of Illinois's splendid library. Enlarging access as well as exclusions leavens the mix. It is a singularly American mixture.

Chapter 3

The 1944
G.I. Bill

To link major contours of the Northwest Ordinance and the Homestead and Morrill Acts to the G.I. Bill of Rights of 1944 requires surmounting the objection that the G.I. Bill was not only a wartime law—its proper style is the Servicemen's Readjustment Act—but one that on its face applied only to military veterans. Some historians insist that attempts of the Roosevelt administration to link veterans' benefits with general policies failed, that the G.I. Bill is only a veterans' measure, not a direct general subsidy of education or housing.[1] An alternative judgment is also feasible. It is that the G.I. Bill transcended its wartime, veterans-only content and contexts and belongs in the Northwest Ordinance–Homestead/Morrill heritage of general social policy.

The G.I. Bill continued the prewar New Deal's essential purpose, "to preserve our economic system," in Eleanor Roosevelt's description, a purpose analogizable back to Ezra Stile's plea of 1783 for a "democratic policy for millions [of Americans], standing upon a broad base of the people at large, amply charged with property."[2] This enlarged context and brave purpose allowed Congressmen of 1944 to resolve a deeply troubling problem familiar to policy makers of 1787 and 1862. The problem: Should military veterans be a specially rewarded, separated class of the population?

Since Homer's *Odyssey* told us of Ulysses' homecoming to Ithaca, the answer in other societies has been almost totally affirmative. But with relatively minor exceptions the American response to Johnny when he comes marching home from our wars has been negative. This tradition appeared to receive the confirmation of success as, after Appomattox, veterans merged easily into the body politic, a process the access laws encouraged. By the 1890s and early 1900s, however, class and social strains attending shifts from quill pens to typewriters, from cottage crafts to smokestack industries, and from frontier homesteads to cities had greatly enlarged worries about social cohesion. After the Spanish-American War and World War I, Congresses and presidents again refused to separate military veterans from the general population in terms of special benefits, including those of access to land, education, and legal remedies, despite strenuous pressures by veterans' lobbies. Some Allied governments subsidized rural cooperatives for their veterans after World War I. But collectives were politically anathema in "first Red Scare" America. In any event, most American war veterans, including many former farmers, preferred urban or suburban comforts to the rigors of agriculture. Congress did extend the 1862 Homestead Act to World War I veterans in 1920. But by the end of that decade, disillusioned and often displaced farmer-veterans had preceded the rest of the nation into the Great Depression and derided these "heartbreak farms" that John Steinbeck described in *The Grapes of Wrath*.

Overall, World War I veterans won only preferential civil service employment and vocational rehabilitation for the physically disabled. Presidents Wilson through Hoover blocked money bonuses for them, a refusal culminating in the violent suppression of the 1929 "bonus marchers." Such thin categories of benefits reached nothing like the magnitudes of the 1787 and 1862–63 access laws, which embraced veterans but primarily as part of the eligible citizenry, and which in terms of landholding, literacy, and legal stability had tried to design or redesign the American dream.[3] After cutting even these sparse benefits in a 1933

New Deal economy move, Roosevelt told angry American Legionnaires "that no person, because he wore a uniform, must thereafter be placed in a special class of beneficiaries over and above all other citizens."[4]

Brave words. But ten years later the United States became involved in a second world war that by every measure exceeded any precedent. A "Depression psychosis" still afflicted most Americans even though the war finally ended unemployment. Pundits worried if democracy, federalism, and capitalism could survive military victory. In an age of militarized totalitarianisms, could or would the sixteen million American military volunteers and draftees merge pacifically into the civilian population?

In 1940, the first peacetime conscription law in America provided that veterans enjoy a right to reemployment in former jobs, a right, supporters of the bill insisted, embraced by the authority of the Constitution to Congress (Article III, Section 8) "To raise and support armies." Then in mid-1942, militarily the darkest time in American history since 1862, FDR encouraged what, two years later, became the G.I. Bill of Rights. It eventually included provisions for reemployment, unemployment compensation, social security, education, and loan guarantees for homes, farms, and businesses, but not homesteading; its day had largely passed. FDR disguised this pioneeringly comprehensive social engineering package in a recommendation from the joint armed services. The G.I. Bill shifted the nature of discussion on Capitol Hill from the Depression psychosis, or a veteran's bonus, to positive alternatives about the desirable limits of government responsibility in reforms, arguments the prewar New Deal had made familiar.

This familiarity is significant. By 1943 anti–New Deal conservatives had obliterated the despised Works Progress Administration (including the Federal Writers' Project) and National Youth Administration, plus other New Deal relief improvisations, especially in areas of cultural enrichment and social welfare. But, in what became the G.I. Bill, administration stalwarts plus congressional liberals, with strong White House support, successfully preserved, by wrapping them in Old Glory, an alphabet soup of basic prewar reforms. Even early drafts of what became "the" G.I. Bill mixed the proposed aid to veterans, especially in education, with both antiunemployment and social improvement goals involving loans to veterans for purchases of homes, farms, and businesses, greatly transcending mere returns to the *status quo ante bellum*. Social security, labor relations, and Federal Housing Administration and Farm Credit Administration loan guarantees for homeowners, farmers, and businessmen became intrinsic elements of the G.I. Bill (elements the creative essence of which appears to elude policymakers of the recessionary 1980s). Thus, though a war measure, the G.I. Bill vastly reinforced these enduring New Deal "civilian" legacies. This linkage of peacetime to wartime public policy commitments allowed unprecedented numbers and segments of the population to enjoy improved access to education, land (housing), and legal remedies. The modern Ulysses was indeed to find a welcome home.

So doing, he built himself a better home. For the first time since the Homestead and Morrill Acts of 1862, planning for the postwar had preceded rather than followed demobilization.[5] This planning culminated in the G.I. Bill, which, plus the hangover New Deal legislation with which it interacted, served to blunt the appeal of a class-based workers' political party in America.

The United States is the only populous industrial, urbanized nation that has not developed such a political party, a singularity that perennially puzzles and even offends some commentators.[6] Instead, continuingly viable and adaptable, the two-party umbrella still serves our complex federal arrangements, democratic politics, and economic capitalism. The degree to which our two-party politics have absorbed industrial workers and marginal farmers, and their acceptance of middle-class attitudes and values, is reflected in the fact that our fiction writers have all but locked them out. Novelists and playwrights including Jack London, Lincoln Steffens, John Dos Passos, Irving Stone, and John Steinbeck had occasionally exhibited warm interest in sweaty heroes. But this concern has virtually disappeared except in macho films and on TV. Perhaps this shrinking of serious interest reflects our continuing acceptance of a success ethic that prefers upwardly mobile Horatio Algers, however humble, to stick-in-the-farm-mud Tom Joads or unambitious urban blue collars like Archie Bunker.[7]

But even the millions of Archie Bunkers, who preferred to return after World War II to the familiar immobility of a factory loading dock workplace, exploited the G.I. Bill or its related statutes to acquire much-improved housing, and moved into the middle class. Creators of the G.I. Bill allowed its former military beneficiaries to choose between Veterans Administration loan provisions or to exploit surviving "civilian" New Deal loan programs such as the Federal Housing Administration or Farm Credit Administration for loan guarantees, both administered on the borrowers' level by private banks, or seek private bank loans entirely. By 1955, almost four million American Ulysses had taken advantage of the home loan provisions either directly under the G.I. Bill or provided by the related federal laws that survived because of it and could still serve non-veterans.[8]

Urban and suburban housing became the substitute of the G.I. Bill for the encouragements to agrarian lifestyles that the Northwest Ordinance and the Homestead Act had offered. Un-Turnerian new frontiers developed along freeways, the latter themselves the very symbol of the brave new postwar world. Consolidated grade schools and proliferating shopping malls attracted capital and populations, with profound consequences for inner-city ghettoes, cities' tax bases, and the environment.

The very contours of public policy had to adapt to changing life-styles, adaptations that modernized—or failed to modernize—American government and reform.[9]

The very changes, the augmented mobility, the swelling demands for civil rights, and the technological displacements of the postwar decades, were deplored by Archie Bunker-ish G.I. Bill beneficiaries in housing and encouraged by others in education, symbolized by the eggheady son-in-law. To carry this imagery on a bit, the Bunkers were content in their G.I. Bill mortgage-burdened housing in a close-in urban development that was vastly superior to prewar rentals. But many "Bunkers," like the white "townies" of Boston and their analogs everywhere, bitterly opposed racial integration of schools and workplaces. Such stubborn opponents to race equality insisted that stable community (i.e., racial, ethnic, religious) values were more important than individuals' mobility and success, an ethic in which a mix of status anxiety and race prejudice seemed to be evident.[10]

Not so the Bunkers' sons-in-law, whether military veterans or not. Hangover New Deal policies and the G.I. Bill opened for such multitudes access to heretofore-unwelcoming universities and degree programs leading to professional careers and away from blue-collar constraints. These very institutions had become enlarged and improved from the effects of these laws. Whole new university systems even included low-tuition urban campuses. The civil rights revolutions from the 1950s through the 1970s reflected the persistent activism of old champions of equality in these enhanced academic environments and the aggressive freshness of the hordes of youthful recruits on campuses, faculty and students alike, to good causes.

Bunker and his son-in-law moved into the middle class. The convulsive efforts of our political parties to corral the support of this new, enlarged middle class remains one of the incomplete dramas of the 1980s.

What is this middle class? As with such concepts as federalism, objectivity, or ideology, answers remain imprecise. Scholars have concentrated during the past forty years more on elites and workers than on the middle class, and on exclusions, discriminations, and prejudices, especially for reasons of race, religion, and gender, more than on access. This concentration has paid off in important insights and analyses. But, in Mary Ryan's apt phrases, the middle class of professionals and businessmen has remained "largely a residual category in American historiography, the assumed, but largely unexamined, context for much of the writing about popular culture and reform movements. . . . Historians have hardly begun to analyze middle Americans as a class unto themselves."[11]

But serious multi-disciplinary inquiries into the very psyche of the entrepreneur have begun, and in happily eclectic manner. Quantifier Richard Jensen agrees that "no satisfactory history of urban America is possible without knowledge of the business and professional leaders in the cities."[12] What Burton Bledstein called "the advantage of being middle class" centered on perceptions and practices of access, especially to higher education.[13]

We need far more information than we now possess about our restlessly mobile, risk-taking, voting, litigating, entrepreneurial center. As Lee Bensen has stressed, the self-consciousness of the middle class in encouraging social and geographical mobility, equality under law, broad income ranges, and well-developed communications and literacy alone justifies attention to this shadowy category.[14]

Stuart Blumin's recent provocative exploration into the processes of middle-class formulation underscored the importance of thrift, sobriety, and application, especially in education and capital accumulation. "The implication," Blumin wrote, ". . . is that the sequence was self-perpetuating—that once implemented these [middle class] strategies would succeed in gaining or securing each family's position in the middle class, and established middle class families would be the ones most likely to pursue the same strategies in subsequent generations." The G.I. Bill built on and greatly expanded what David Levine has called the American "culture of aspiration" that had already developed in elite private colleges and in state land-grant institutions before World War II.[15]

Education has allowed the pursuit. Especially in the realm of higher education, the G.I. Bill proved to be a surprising success. Millions—eventually, eight million—of World War II (and Korean War) veterans undertook educational or training programs under it. Not all of these enrollees sought undergraduate degrees and, fewer still, graduate degrees. But the numbers that did become college graduates, M.A.s, and Ph.D.s, plus equivalents in the science and professional curricula, revolutionized the American university structure and professoriat. It is very difficult even to imagine a pre–World War II participation by academics in a civil rights march from Selma to Montgomery, Alabama, or anywhere else, and in other demands of the 1960s for race equality. Similarly, the much more courageous stands of universities and faculty against demagogues during the post–World War II "second Red Scare" hysteria, as compared to the first Red Scare of the 1920s, and the contrast between the careers of W. E. B. Du Bois and John Hope Franklin owes something to the greatly democratized university systems of our time.[16]

The expanded higher education systems that many public and private universities developed, often after great and determined foot dragging by long-overprivileged land-grant or state campuses in their bucolic retreats, and the growth of community colleges, reflect the surge to postsecondary alternatives that the G.I. Bill opened. Universities, long the haven of elites, became major instruments of democratic service and of merging military veterans into civilian pursuits. Education and housing blended aspirations and ubiquitized opportunities.

For some uncountable number of veterans, the G.I. Bill made reasonable the pursuit of careers that, before the war, were unrealistic even if perceived, and that older siblings simply never aspired to. Customary exclusions based on ethnic and religious bigotries broke down. Even history Ph.D. seminars admitted their first Jews and Catholics between 1945 and 1950, along with their first blacks. Asians, Hispanics, and females followed in their wakes.

The seriousness and diligence of former military students infected the nonveterans and perhaps the faculty as well. The competition veterans offered to nonveteran students swiftened the pace of classrooms. Campus dialogue grew more intense. One commentator, an enthusiast about the G.I. Bill, concluded that by 1950 higher education had eventually to take stock of itself by reason of the more critical standards and more demanding attitudes of students, veterans and nonveterans alike.[17]

Presidents of elite universities including Harvard and Chicago had fought the G.I. Bill, as Charles Eliot Norton once opposed the Morrill Act. Unable to kill it, they tried to restrict its higher education benefits only to exceptionally qualified veteran applicants whose educations the war had interrupted. Any mass invasion of campuses by less-well-prepared exotics would deteriorate standards and overstrain faculties, libraries, and laboratories, ran the refrain. Such critics of the approaches of the G.I. Bill preferred a postwar educational universe little different from the prewar.

It was not to be. These lobbyists failed to appreciate the capacity of education to beget education, and by the begetting to improve it and the society as a whole.

By 1960 this general escalation inspired one writer to suggest that "the G.I. Bill challenged social stratification. It reopened

society's clogged channels. Large numbers of veterans who before the war had been [fixed] in relatively low-paid occupations
moved upward to much higher paying jobs and to the professions."[18]

The move did not directly or soon enough apply to blacks and
other disfavored minorities. The G.I. Bill did not include a bar
against race discrimination, although FDR and Harry Truman
pushed race integration in the military and civil services. Lack-
ing an antidiscrimination ban, and leaving the disbursement of
funds to state authorities, the G.I. Bill in effect subsidized continuing and enlarging disproportions between the incomes of
white public colleges and universities, and the A&Is and A&Ms
that in some states equaled the label *black*. But it is also true, as
noted earlier, that the years of the G.I. Bill's implementation led
also to the years of the "civil rights revolution," a revolution that
focused on more equal access to housing, education, and legal
remedies for all Americans.

Out of it all sensitivity grew to these bedrock questions
of justice and access, a sensitivity reflected in major Supreme
Court decisions that from New Deal days shaped our lives. Two
generations of constitutional law and history, and law students,
have had to immerse themselves in *Shelley* v. *Kraemer*, a 1948
ruling that private, racially restrictive real estate covenants were
judicially unenforceable, and in a companion ruling (*Hurd* v.
Hodge) that such covenants in the District of Columbia con-
travened the 1866 Civil Rights Act. Race barriers to housing
(land) cracked a little.

In the 1950s and 1960s, responsive new statutes and judicial
decisions on civil rights, including those that further enlarged
access to federal courts in rights-connected litigations and appeals, became almost superhighways of social control through
litigation. Reformers, in effect, enlisted litigation to implement
legislation. Social control through lawsuits is an old story in

America. Increased access to education, property (housing), and legal remedies by judicial decisions is relatively recent and beneficent, despite the concerns of present Chief Justice of the United States Warren Burger who complains frequently that court dockets are logjammed and jurists overtasked by such burdens. His propositions generate little excitement or widespread belief.

Race barriers to education also began to crack as result of high court decisions back in 1938, when the Court, in a Missouri case (*Missouri ex. rel. Gaines* v. *Canada*), decided that a state, denying equal if segregated in-state law education for one of its black citizens, violated the Fourteenth Amendment. By 1948 this Missouri case was itself a precedent for the similar if constrained *Sipuel* decision of the Court from Oklahoma. Evasions by that state of the Fourteenth Amendment, in terms of segregating a single black law student behind curtains, and further evasions by Texas in terms of establishing for one Negro student a wholly separate and theoretically equal law school, received condemnations from the whole Court in the 1950 decisions *Sweatt* v. *Painter* and *Laurin* v. *Oklahoma*. Four years later the question of segregated elementary education in Kansas came to the Court with *Brown* v. *Board of Education*.

Nothing has since been the same. Such judicial verdicts and the upsurge in levels of life and labor that the G.I. Bill and related programs fueled made the 1960s and the 1970s decades of high aspirations and achievements for social justice and individual fulfillment. Federal judges, rediscovering even partially the proper purposes of the Thirteenth and Fourteenth Amendments, helped to create this revolution, to the benefit of all American society. Diverse and complex, the politics of desegregation in higher education are illuminated by the black landgrant institution in Maryland. It began as a Freedmen's Bureau school, then, as the Princess Anne Academy, it brought the state federal money under the 1890 amendment to the Morrill Act.

But until the 1950s, the University of Maryland grabbed most of the funds. Then the "academy" became the University of Maryland, Eastern Shore, and the flagship campus could no longer monopolize Morrill Act income.

In Tennessee, the flagship state university kept "historically black" Tennessee State University subordinated. Then in 1977 a federal court order merged TSU with the new, budgetarily over-favored Nashville campus of the University of Tennessee, the latter itself a product of judicial decisions requiring fairer shakes for urban citizens.[19]

Texas reversed the Tennessee pattern. In 1883 the state assigned to the then-infant University of Texas two million acres of seeming wasteland as its endowment. But since 1923 over $2 billion of oil royalties swelled the Permanent Improvement Fund at the university. Only in the early 1980s could competing Morrill Act universities in Texas, Texas A&M and traditionally black Prairie View A&M, and the more recently established University of Houston and Texas Southern University, squeeze proportional shares of oil income from UT and fairer shares of tax resources from state lawmakers, who were often alumni of the overadvantaged University of Texas and Texas A&M. Of the less-favored institutions, Texas Southern University resulted from the Supreme Court decision in *Sweatt* v. *Painter*. It duplicates degree programs, faculty, libraries, and other facilities on the physically neighboring campus of the University of Houston. But political realities and race pride (Barbara Jordan, the now-professor ex-Congresswoman from Texas, is a TSU alumna) make merger highly improbable, however more efficient, economical, and prestigious a merged university might be.[20]

My word processor has taped to it a line from T. S. Eliot's last *Quartet*: "The end of our exploring will be to arrive where we started and see the place for the first time." So advised, I have attempted, in order to inquire about the singularity of aspects in experiences of this society, to explore, as if "for the first time," Revolutionary and early national America. I found that numerous connections existed between the exceptional Northwest Ordinance and the Declaration of Independence and the Constitution. These connections took me to other singular contemporary enactments such as the first Judiciary Act. From there I advanced to Civil War and Reconstruction America, especially to the 1862 Morrill and Homestead Acts and the Thirteenth and Fourteenth Amendments of 1865 and 1868, respectively, and then to the 1944 G.I. Bill of World War II and its ennobling heir, *Brown v. Board of Education.*

Such reviews have recruited me for that increasing cadre of colleagues who are reaffirming American exceptionalism, at least for the aspects of our history to which I have attempted to attend. These reestimations tend to confirm a view that we are not, as my Rice University colleague Allen Matusow suggested, experiencing an "unraveling" of America.[21]

Instead, eclectic information in addition to the phenomena I have sketched, substantiates alternative views. Synthesizing a large body of technical reports, one recent *New York Times* writer concluded that after twenty years, the education programs of the Great Society, themselves deriving from imperatives I have tried to describe, are "a solid legacy" to the 1980s. And, writing on the American way of death, William Rathje, observing the present increasing ostentation of funeral arrangements even by "ordinary folk," wondered if this ostentation does not suggest also "a blurring of class distinctions, which in turn implies a high degree of social mobility and economic vitality [a] linkage [that] occurs in diverse cultures and throughout history." It may be, Rathje continued, that a future anthropologist, deriving evidence about our times from our cemeteries, may infer justifiably that however "hideous, pretentious, and unprincipled" the "American way of Death was in the 1980s, . . . the gaudy accoutrements of death are . . . clues to later generations that our society was relatively egalitarian and robust. This, to my mind, is the message of the orbiting mausoleum. Alive or dead, it seems to say, in America you have a shot at upward mobility."[22]

So it seems to me. We may not be the excited, hopeful society of 1945 or 1954. The ebullient 1960s and itchy 1970s are behind us. Our problems of economic and industrial transitions, hardcore unemployment and welfare population, and diminishing potency in international affairs, especially concerning private and/or officially inspired terrorisms, remain unsolved. Other concerns, including abortion, health services, gender and race equality, and civil liberties, almost daily take on unanticipated and more complex shadings. But healthy enlargements of our civil rights agendas are not, arguably, steps toward fragmentation.

As the bicentennial of our Constitution nears, neither major political party exhibits a capacity to innovate in these matters anywhere close to the levels reached in 1787 with the Northwest Ordinance, in 1862 with the Morrill and Homestead Acts, or in 1944 with the G.I. Bill. These laws were the products of our most liberating thinker-politicians, and it is impressive that the Morrill Act is gaining respect and reconsideration in 1985 (*New York Times*, November 3, 1985; op. ed. page) as a model for a network between industry and universities that might again help America gain a market edge in international trade. Liberalism has always had its challengers. But it is unsettling to find its present challengers not only in the White House, but, as importantly, in the implementing agencies including the lower federal courts. These administrative and judicial agencies at the throttles of our access agenda are, it appears, staffed with appointees who seem frequently to misread our constitutional and legal history.[23]

If Willard Hurst was correct, the historically validated uses of throttles in our national experience have been to release energy for useful purposes, not to choke it off. Choking analogies exist between civil rights policies of the Reagan Administration and

Andrew Johnson's sustained and tragically successful obstacles to implementations of the 1865 Freedmen's Bureau law and the 1866 Civil Rights Act. Can we stand another century-long, or even decade-long deferred commitment to equality?

We cannot change the past. But we can improve our understanding of it. The *Brown* decision of 1954 was as essentially correct on historical grounds as on those of specific constitutional duty and general morality; that is, during the Civil War, Americans had forced open roads to their futures and ours, including some that involved biracial and gender-blind equality of access to land, education, and legal remedies. Supreme Court Justices of the 1870s and later helped to close off those new roads. In the 1950s other justices reopened them. What will future Russell Lecturers, perhaps those at the tricentennial of the Constitution, say of the 1980s?

With which query I close, with an approach to wisdom offered by the poet Auden. He advised us that History is the "madonna of silences / To whom we turn / When we have lost control"; she into whose eyes "we look for recognition / After we have been found out." And, last, a question by the "beat generation" poet, Jack Kerouac: "Whither goest thou America, in thy shiny new car?"

Notes

Acknowledgments

1. H. M. Hyman, "Not Cassandra, Pandora, or Polonius: Learning, Technology, and Law in American History" (Paper delivered at State of Colorado Conference on Technology and Learning, Denver, Oct. 1983).
2. Lamb to Waite, Oct. 13, 1875, Waite Papers, Manuscripts Division, Library of Congress.

Introduction

1. Matusow, *The Unraveling of America: A History of Liberalism in the 1960s* (1984). See also Kirk F. Koerner, *Liberalism and Its Critics* (1985).
2. Berger and Podhoretz in *New York Times*, May 5, 1985, E 18, Y 9; Bellow in *New York Times*, January 15, 1986, Y 19; On the Critical Legal Studies movement, see William E. Nelson and John P. Reid, *The Literature of American Legal History* (1985), chap. 16. See also Clelak, *America's Quest for the Ideal Self: Dissent and Fulfillment in the 60s and 70s* (1985); Chafe, *The Unfinished Journey: America Since World War II* (1985).
3. White, "On Intellectual Gloom," *American Scholar* 35 (1966): 223.
4. A mugwump is a bird with his head on one side of the fence and his wump on the other.
5. Morison, "Faith of a Historian," *American Historical Review* 56 (1951): 272; and see Thomas J. Pressly, *Americans Interpret Their Civil War* (1962), 302.
6. WASP equals white Anglo-Saxon Protestant, at least in commonplace use. I acknowledge Richard Frost's letter to the editor protest, *Journal of American History* 72 (1985): 483, that "all Anglo-Saxons are white" and, therefore, WASP is redundant. Yes, but too useful to abandon.
7. H. M. Hyman, ed., *The Radical Republicans and Reconstruction, 1861–1870* (1966), intro.

8. Christopher Jencks and David Riesman, *The Academic Revolution* (1968), esp. chaps. 2 and 12; Norman Cantor, "The Real Crisis in the Humanities Today," *New Criterion* 3 (1985): 28.

9. Morison, "Faith of a Historian," 266–67, 272; Pressly, *Americans Interpret*, 302.

10. A. R. Millett and P. Maslowski, *For the Common Defense: A Military History of the United States of America* (1984), is an example, and offers copious ideas and bibliography.

11. Charles Murray, *Losing Ground: American Social Policy, 1950–80* (1984); A. Arblaster, *The Rise and Decline of Western Liberalism* (1984).

12. Parish, "American History Arrives in Europe," *New York Times Book Review*, Feb. 3, 1985, 1; Lasch, *The Minimal Self: Psychic Survival in Troubled Times* (1984).

13. Ruth Elson, *Guardians of Tradition: American Schoolbooks of the Nineteenth Century* (1964); R. Wiebe, "Social Functions of Public Education," *American Quarterly* 21 (1969): 147; Frances Fitzgerald, *America Revised* (1979).

14. D. D. Van Tassel, "From Learned Society to Professional Organization: The American Historical Association, 1884–1900," *American Historical Review* 89 (1984): 929.

15. Morison, "Faith of a Historian," 272.

16. D. J. Singal, "Beyond Consensus: Richard Hofstadter and American Historiography," *American Historical Review* 89 (1984): 976.

17. J. M. McPherson, "Antebellum Southern Exceptionalism: A New Look at an Old Question," *Civil War History* 29 (1983): 230; Laurence Veysey, "The Autonomy of American History Reconsidered," *American Quarterly* 31 (1979): 455–77.

18. Parish, "American History," 1, 28–29.

19. Higham, "Beyond Consensus: The Historian as Moral Critic," *American Historical Review* 67 (1962): 609; Gordon Wright, "History as a Moral Science," *American Historical Review* 81 (1976): 1.

20. William R. Thayer, ed., *Life and Letters of John Hay*, 2 vols. (1908), 2: 33.

21. H. M. Hyman, "Is American Federalism Still a Fundamental Value?" in R. Jeffrys-Jones and Bruce Collins, eds., *The Growth of Federal Power in American History* (1983), 143–56; H. M. Hyman, "Clio and Mars: Happy Bedmates?" *Organization of American Historians Newsletter* (Feb., 1984), 5–7; J. Kimball, "The Influence of Ideology on Interpretive Disagreement," *History Teacher* (1984), 355.

22. Handlin, *Truth in History* (1979), 110.

23. T. Dennett, ed., *Lincoln and the Civil War in the Diaries and Letters of John Hay* (1939), 139, 205; Lincoln, *Collected Works*, 9 vols., ed. Roy P. Basler (1953), 8: 403.

24. Beard, "Written History as an Act of Faith," *American Historical Review* 39 (1934): 219; Degler, "Remaking American History," *Journal of American History* 67 (1980): 7.

25. Pole, *The Pursuit of Equality in America* (1978).

26. Fred Mathews, "The Reassertion of American Exceptionalism: From Progressivism to Liberalism in the Intellectual Weeklies, 1920–1950" (Paper delivered to annual meeting of the Southern Historical Association, 1985), offers an overview of literary reflections of the theme. I thank the author for his kindness in providing me with an advance copy.

27. Deutsch, "The Growth of Nations," *World Politics* 5 (1953): 169.

28. Harold Berman's *Law and Revolution: The Formation of the Western Legal Tradition* (1983) is an outstanding example of integration of data and analysis.

29. See, e.g., M. Schoenfeld and J. R. Mock, "Benefits for Ex-Servicemen in Five British Countries and the U.S.," *Monthly Labor Review* (Nov. 1945): 900; President's Commission on Veterans' Pensions, *Canadian Benefits for War Veterans: Comparison with U.S. Veterans' Benefits* (House Committee Print 259, 84 Cong., 2 sess., 1956); U.S. Cong., House, "Survey of Benefits Granted to Veterans by Foreign Countries" (Committee Print 169, 86 Cong., 2 sess., 1960).

30. P. Sharp, "Three Frontiers: Some Comparative Studies of Canadian, American, and Australian Settlement," *Pacific Historical Review* 24 (1955): 369; Walker Wyman and C. Kroeber, eds., *Frontier in Perspective* (1957). See also *Harvard Guide to American History*, 2 vols. (1974 ed.), 1: 344, 508, and passim.

31. J. D. Richardson, ed., *Messages and Papers of the Presidents* 10 vols. (1901), 6: 142, 191.

32. Perry, *The Constitution, the Courts, and Human Rights* (1982), 75.

33. Bender, "Making History Whole Again," *New York Times Book Review*, Oct. 6, 1985, 1, 42–43.

34. Pole, *The Gift of Government: Political Responsibility from the English Restoration to American Independence* (1983).

35. Commager, *The Empire of Reason: How Europe Imagined and Americans*

Realized the Enlightenment (1977); Carl L. Becker, *The Heavenly City of the Eighteenth-Century Philosophers* (1932).

36. David Tyack generously afforded me access to the typescript of a book he is coauthoring with Thomas James and Aaron Benavot on the legal history of American public education, a book tentatively titled: *Law in the History of the Public Schools* (to be published by the University of Wisconsin Press, 1986). I derive some of these insights from chap. 1 of this draft. See also Bernard Bailyn, *Education in the Forming of American Society* (1960).

37. R. C. Stuart, *War and American Thought: From the Revolution to the Monroe Doctrine* (1982), intro. and chap. 1.

38. James T. Johnson, *The Just War Tradition and the Restraint of War* (1983).

Chapter 1. The 1787 Northwest Ordinance

1. McPherson, "Antebellum Southern Exceptionalism: A New Look at an Old Question," *Civil War History* 29 (1983): 230.

2. Jensen, *The New Nation: A History of the United States During the Confederation, 1781–1789* (1950), 354; cf. Julian P. Boyd, "Jefferson's 'Empire of Liberty,'" *Virginia Quarterly Review* 24 (1948): 583.

3. Quotations in, respectively, Peter Onuf, "A Constitution for New States," (Paper delivered at Claremont (Calif.) Institute Conference, Feb., 1984), 31; Onuf, "From Constitution to Higher Law: The Reinterpretation of the Northwest Ordinance," *Ohio History* 94 (1985): 32.

4. Carstensen, ed., *The Public Lands: Studies in the History of the Public Domain*, (1962), xxv–xxvi.

5. R. S. Hill, Peter Onuf, and other members of the Northwest Ordinance Bicentennial Planning Committee generously supplied research papers and other data. See also William B. Scott, *In Pursuit of Happiness: American Conceptions of Property from the Seventeenth to the Twentieth Century* (1977); Fred Mathews, "The Reassertion of American Exceptionalism: From Progressivism to Liberalism in the Intellectual Weeklies, 1920–1950" (Paper delivered at Southern Historical Association annual meeting, 1985).

6. Billington, *Westward Expansion* (1949), 217; Bailyn *et al.*, *The Great*

Republic (1977), 304; Bailyn and Morgan in *Essays on the American Revolution*, eds. S. G. Kurtz and J. H. Hutson (1973), 20, 306–7.

7. Onuf, "From Constitution to Higher Law," 32; Onuf, "Settlers, Settlements, and States: The Origins of the American Territorial System" (Paper delivered at Johns Hopkins University, 1985).

8. May 11, 1786, in Julian P. Boyd, ed., *The Papers of Thomas Jefferson*, 20 vols. to date (1950–) 9:51.

9. Berkhofer, "Providing for the Expansion of a Republican Empire: From Jefferson's Ordinance of 1784 to the Northwest Ordinance of 1787" (Paper delivered to annual meeting of the Organization of American Historians, 1968); Berkhofer, "Northwest Ordinance and the Principles of Territorial Evolution," in John Bloom, ed., *American Territorial System* (1983), 45–55.

10. Undated, quoted in Dixon Wecter, *When Johnny Comes Marching Home* (1944), 47; Davis R. B. Ross, *Preparing for Ulysses: Politics and Veterans During World War II* (1969), intro.

11. Wecter, *When Johnny Comes Marching Home*, 47–100; Feller, *The Public Lands in Jacksonian Politics* (1984), 197–98.

12. Wiebe, *The Opening of American Society from the Adoption of the Constitution to the Eve of Disunion* (1984), 129. See also Jefferson's *Notes on the State of Virginia* (1782).

13. Onuf, "Liberty, Development, and Union: Visions of the West in the 1780s," (Paper delivered at Liberty Fund Conference, 1985); Major L. Wilson, *Space, Time, and Freedom* (1974); Lawrence J. Friedman, *Inventors of the Promised Land* (1975), esp. 3–43; Rush Welter, *Popular Education and Democratic Thought in America* (1962), chap. 2.

14. A. R. L. Clayton, "Planning the Republic: The Federalists and Internal Improvements in the Old Northwest," (Paper delivered to annual meeting of the Organization of American Historians, 1985), 10.

15. G. S. Fainsford, *Congress and Higher Education in the Nineteenth Century* (1971), 36 n. 20; chaps. 1–2.

16. Eldon L. Johnson, "Misconceptions About the Early Land-Grant Colleges," *Journal of Higher Education* 52 (1981): 334.

17. Young, "Congress Looks West: Liberal Ideology and Public Land Policy in the Nineteenth Century," in D. M. Ellis, ed., *The Frontier in American Development* (1969), 74.

18. Berkhofer, "Providing for the Expansion of a Republican Empire."

19. Appleby, *Capitalism and a New Social Order* (1984), 16 and passim.

20. Nash, Review of *Essays on the American Revolution*, ed. by Stephen G.

Kurtz and James H. Hutson, *William and Mary Quarterly* 31 (3d ser., 1974): 311–14; *ibid.*, 32 (1975), 182–85; Lawrence S. Wittner, "Pursuing the 'National Interest': The Illusion of Realism," *Reviews in American History* 13, (1985): 284; R. S. Hill, "The Northwest Ordinance and the French Slaves," and Finkelman, "Slavery, the Northwest Ordinance, and the Founding Fathers," (Papers delivered at Claremont (Calif.) Institute Conference, Feb. 1984); *Irredeemable America: The Indians' Estate and Land Claims*, ed. Imre Sutton (1985), 3–70 passim.

21. Finkelman, *An Imperfect Union: Slavery, Federalism, and Comity* (1983); H. M. Hyman and W. M. Wiecek, *Equal Justice Under Law: Constitutional Development, 1835–1875* (1982), esp. chaps. 4–5, 10–11.

22. Wallace Farnham, "The Weakened Spring of Government," *American Historical Review* 68 (1963): 662; William E. Nelson, *Roots of American Bureaucracy, 1830–1900* (1982), chaps. 1–2.

23. L. M. Friedman, "The Law Between the States: Some Thoughts on Southern Legal History," in D. J. Bodenhamer and James W. Ely, Jr., eds., *Ambivalent Legacy* (1984), 30.

24. Rakove, "Ironies of Empire: Hope, Desperation, and the Making of the Northwest Ordinance," (Paper delivered at Claremont (Calif.) Institute Conference, Feb. 1985), esp. p. 4 and n.; Avins, "Black Studies, White Separation, and Reflected Light on College Segregation and the Fourteenth Amendment from Early Land Grant College Policies," *Washburn Law Journal* 10 (1971): 181; William Wiecek, *The Sources of Antislavery Constitutionalism, 1760–1848* (1977).

25. Prince's review of Richard Matthews, *The Radical Politics of Thomas Jefferson: A Revisionist View* (1984), in *Journal of American History* 72 (1985): 395.

26. Davis, in Ira Berlin and Ronald Hoffman, eds., *Slavery and Freedom in the Age of the American Revolution* (1983), 279–80; see also his *The Problem of Slavery in the Age of Revolution, 1770–1823* (1975), 503 and passim.

27. Davis, *Slavery and Human Progress* (1984).

28. Onuf, "From Constitution to Higher Law," 5, 30–33.

29. Dane, *General Abridgement and Digest of American Law,* 9 vols. (1829) 9: iv; Andrew J. Johnson, "Life and Constitutional Thought of Nathan Dane," (Ph.D. diss., Indiana University, 1964).

30. Howe, *Justice Oliver Wendell Holmes: The Proving Years* (1963), 201.

31. Berkhofer, "Providing for the Expansion of a Republican Empire."

32. Frankfurter and Landis, *The Business of the Supreme Court* (1928), 4.

33. M. K. Bonsteel Tachau, *Federal Courts in the Early Republic* (1978);

Richard Ellis, *The Jeffersonian Crisis: Courts and Politics in the Young Republic* (1971), esp. chaps. 1, 16.

34. Wiebe, *Opening of American Society,* 135; Nevins, *The State Universities and Democracy* (1962), 21 and chap. 1.

35. Fred Mathews, " 'Hobbesian Populism': Interpretive Paradigms and Moral Vision in American Historiography," *Journal of American History* 72 (1985): 92, 98, esp. n. 10.

36. A. Fede, "Toward a Solution of the Slave Law Dilemma: A Critique of Tushnet's 'The American Law of Slavery'," *Law and History Review* 2 (1984): 301.

Chapter 2. The 1862 Homestead and Morrill Acts

1. H. M. Hyman and W. M. Wiecek, *Equal Justice Under Law: Constitutional Development, 1835–1875* (1982), chaps. 4–5, 9–10.

2. See also G. N. Rainsford, *Congress and Higher Education in the Nineteenth Century* (1971), 96–97.

3. *Statutes at Large of the United States,* 12: 755.

4. W. M. Wiecek, "The Reconstruction of Federal Judicial Power, 1863–1876," *American Journal of Legal History* 13 (1969): 333.

5. A. Avins, "Black Studies, White Separation, and Reflected Light on College Segregation and the Fourteenth Amendment from Early Land Grant College Policies," *Washburn Law Journal* 10 (1971): 181.

6. Katz interviewed in *New York Times,* May 3, 1983: (quoted in Stephen Botein, "Scientific Mind and Legal Matter." *Reviews in American History* 13 [1985]: 315) and see *Times* (Oct. 13, 1985), 1, for parallel views by Justice William Brennan.

7. Hyman and Wiecek, *Equal Justice Under Law,* 222–23.

8. Avins, "Black Studies," 181, esp. 211; J. Lurie, "The Fourteenth Amendment: Use and Application in Selected State Court Civil Liberties Cases, 1870–1890," *American Journal of Legal History* 28 (1984): 295.

9. Gilmore, *Ages of American Law* (1977), 146.

10. Cf. S. Millet, *Selected Bibliography of American Constitutional History* (1975), and Kermit Hall, *Comprehensive Bibliography of American Constitutional and Legal History, 1896–1979,* 5 vols. (1984); P. Murphy, "Time to Reclaim: The Current Challenge of American Constitu-

tional History," *American Historical Review* 69 (1963): 65; Milton Klein, "Clio and the Law: The Uncertain Promise of American Legal History," (Paper delivered at Fourth Reynolds Conference, University of South Carolina, 1978); Botein, "Scientific Mind and Legal Matter," 303.

11. R. Goodenow and D. Ravitch, eds., *Schools in Cities: Consensus and Conflict in American Educational History* (1983), ix.

12. E. Pessen, "Social Mobility in America: Some Brief Reflections," *Journal of Southern History* 45 (1979): 165; William Cohen, "Black Immobility and Free Labor: The Freedmen's Bureau and the Relocation of Black Labor, 1865–1868," *Civil War History* 30 (1984): 221.

13. Bender, "The New History—Then and Now," *Reviews in American History* 12 (1984): 612, 620–21; Scheiber, "American Constitutional History and the New Legal History: Complementary Themes in Two Modes," *Journal of American History* 68 (1981): 343 n. 31, and 377 n. 1.

14. H. M. Hyman, "Is American Federalism Still a Fundamental Value? Scholars Views in Transition," in R. Jeffreys-Jones and Bruce Collins, eds., *The Growth of Federal Power in American History* (1983), 143.

15. W. Washburn, "The Supreme Court's Use and Abuse of History," Organization of American Historians *Newsletter* (Aug. 1983); J. Wofford, "The Blinding Light: The Uses of History in Constitutional Interpretation," *University of Chicago Law Review* 31 (1964): 502.

16. Pickens, "The Republican Synthesis and Thaddeus Stevens," *Civil War History* 31 (1985): 57.

17. R. J. Kaczorowski, *The Politics of Judicial Interpretation: The Federal Courts, Department of Justice, and Civil Rights, 1866–1876* (1985).

18. Hyman and Wiecek, *Equal Justice Under Law,* chap. 11.

19. Beverly W. Palmer, "From Small Minority to Great Cause: Letters of Charles Sumner to Salmon P. Chase," *Ohio History* 93 (1985): 164.

20. Phillip Bradley et al., eds., *Democracy in America,* 2 vols. (Vintage ed., 1945), 1: 198–99.

21. Hurst, *Law and the Conditions of Freedom in the Nineteenth Century United States* (1956).

22. Lieber to Sumner, Aug. 24, 1865, no. LI3908, box 53, Lieber Papers, Huntington Library.

23. H. M. Hyman, *Quiet Past and Stormy Present? War Powers in American History* (1986).

24. Nelson, *The Roots of American Bureaucracy,* chap. 3; Morton Keller, *Affairs of State* (1977), pt. 1.

25. Scheiber, "American Federalism and the Diffusion of Power," *University of Toledo Law Review* 9 (1978): 619; Miller, "Reconstruction and Revenue: Dilemmas of Federal Law Enforcement in the South, 1870–1885," (Paper delivered to annual meeting of the Organization of American Historians, 1985).

26. Sherman in *Congressional Globe*, 37th Cong., 3d sess., 820–26 (Feb. 9, 1863); M. L. Benedict, "Preserving the Constitution: The Conservative Basis of Radical Reconstruction," *Journal of American History* 61 (1974): 65; H. M. Hyman, *A More Perfect Union*, chaps. 18–19.

27. "Americans and Their Prisons," *Law Magazine and Law Review* 25 (London, 1868): 57–58.

28. McCrary, "The Party of Revolution: Republican Ideas About Politics and Social Change, 1862–1867," *Civil War History* 30 (1984): 330, 350.

29. Louis Gerteis and William Nelson graciously allowed me access to the typescripts of their forthcoming books, Gerteis's on freedom national, and Nelson's on *The Fourteenth Amendment: From Political Principle to Judicial Doctrine*. I thank them both.

30. David Fowler, "Northern Attitudes Toward Interracial Marriage" (Ph.D. diss., Yale University, 1963); John M. Werner, " 'Reaping the Bloody Harvest': Race Riots During the Age of Jackson" (Ph.D. diss., Indiana University, 1972).

31. Kaczorowski, *Politics of Judicial Interpretation*, chaps. 1–3; Hyman and Wiecek, *Equal Justice Under Law*, chap. 11. Judith Baer's *Equality Under the Constitution: Reclaiming the Constitution* (1983) is self-described (p. 13) as "passionate, committed scholarship." It shares in the Critical Legal Studies thrust of imposing authors' present aims on the past. I prefer to have the past speak for itself in terms of its own context. See also Nelson and Reid, *Literature of American Legal History*, 264 and chap. 16, passim. The foregoing embraces with the Morrill Act, the 1887 Hatch Act, establishing agricultural experiment stations, and the 1914 Smith-Lever Act, which established extension programs in agricultural and home economics.

32. Lincoln, *Collected Works*, ed. R. P. Basler, 9 vols. (1953), 7: 55; Hyman, *A More Perfect Union*, 210–11.

33. William Hanchett, *The Lincoln Murder Conspiracies* (1983), 37, 155; H. M. Hyman, "Hitting the Fan(s) Again; or, Sic Semper Conspiracies," *Reviews in American History* (1984), 388; Hyman, *Lincoln's Reconstruction: Neither Failure of Vision Nor Vision of Failure* (1980). Contemporary perception that emancipation was tied to access to

education is evident in such illustrations as J. L. Magee's print entitled "Emancipation," in which Lincoln is depicted as treading on the serpent of evil and the symbolic chain and shackle of slavery and in which black and white beneficiaries look toward a public school, offering "education to all classes," as the symbol of their deliverance. Harold Holzer, Gabor S. Boritt, and Mark E. Neely, Jr., in *Changing the Lincoln Image* (Fort Wayne, Ind., 1985), p. 50, say of this print: "What is most remarkable about this print, of course, is its unprecedented, almost radical universality: this Lincoln is emancipating not only slaves but the starving whites of the ravaged South—something Lincoln himself hoped emancipation would accomplish. Its message was of equal opportunity, equal access to self-improvement. It is unique in the archives of Lincoln print portraiture."

34. Hyman and Wiecek, *Equal Justice Under Law,* chaps. 8–11.

35. Simon, "The Politics of the Morrill Act," *Agricultural History* 37 (1963): 103, 104. Raymond Walter's *Burden of Brown: Thirty Years of School Desegregation* (1984) is, according to Nelson and Reid, *Literature of American Legal History,* 270: "Like most lawyers' legal history, . . . concerned not with historical inquiry into why the past occurred as it did but with an existing line of decisions which, in the author's view, should be modified or overruled."

36. W. Hoffnagle, "The Southern Homestead Act: Its Origins and Operation," *Historian* 32 (1970): 612.

37. Avins, "Black Studies," 213.

38. Douglass to Child, July 30, 1865, in Foner, ed., *Douglas,* 4 vols. (1950–55) 4: 71; Hurd to Lieber, undated (ca. July 1868), no. LI 2422, Lieber Papers, Huntington Library.

39. April 2, 1869, Sumner Papers, vol. 94, no. 4, Houghton Library, Harvard University.

40. R. L. Labb, "New Light on the Slaughterhouse Monopoly Act of 1869," in E. W. Haas, ed., *Louisiana's Legal Heritage* (1983), 143; Hyman and Wiecek, *Equal Justice Under Law,* chaps. 10–12.

41. R. C. Palmer, "The Parameters of Constitutional Reconstruction: Slaughterhouse, Cruikshank, and the Fourteenth Amendment," *University of Illinois Law Review Symposium in Legal History* (1984): 739.

42. In John Higham, "Herbert Baxter Adams and the Study of Local History," *American Historical Review* 89 (1984): 126.

43. In Gene Gressley, "The Turner Thesis—A Problem in Historiography," *Agricultural History* 32 (1958): 227, 229.
44. Potter, *People of Plenty* (1954), 158; D. J. Weber, "Turner, the Boltonians, and the Borderlands," *American Historical Review* 91 (1986): 66.
45. Pp. 68–69. Continuing, Beard asserted that "by a strange fate the energies of individual enterprises thus trained in schools under state and local auspices, and released in action, swiftly rounded out the continent, laced all parts of the country together by systems of transportation, and bound its sections and industries into a national economy. Meanwhile agencies of communication merged provincial ideas and thought into a larger consensus, such as the founders of the Republic had sought to create. So it has come about that public education, as in 1789 [under the Northwest Ordinance], is once more concerned with the national economy and interests, despite its origins in state and local enterprise. The age-long conflict between centralism and particularism, between collective interest and private interest, has not closed, and cannot be closed; but upon educational leadership devolves a . . . responsibility for keeping that conflict within the bounds of exact knowledge . . . and the democratic process, and of contributing to the formation of wise and humane decisions."
46. Gates, "The Homestead Act: Free Land Policy in Operation, 1862–1935," in H. W. Ottoson, ed., *Land Use Policy and Problems in the United States* (1963), 28, 43.
47. See earlier citations to titles by Hurst, Hyman, Keller, Nelson, and Scheiber.
48. Joland Mohr, "Higher Education and the Development of Professionalism in America" (Ph.D. diss., University of Minnesota, 1984).
49. Eldon L. Johnson, "Misconceptions About the Early Land-Grant Colleges," *Journal of Higher Education* 52 (1981): 333, 338–39.
50. See R. P. Hudson, "Abraham Flexner in Perspective: American Medical Education, 1865–1910," *Bulletin of the History of Medicine* 46 (1972): 546.
51. Lawrence Veysey, *The Emergence of the American University* (1967); Talcott Parsons in Edwin R. A. Seligman and Alvin Johnson, eds., *Encyclopedia of the Social Sciences*, 15 vols. (1968), 12: 545.
52. Johnson, "Misconceptions," 338–91.
53. Varg, "The Land Grant Philosophy and Liberal Education," *Centen-*

nial Review 6 (1962): 435, 436, 444; Thomas LeDuc, "History and Appraisal of Land Policy to 1862," in H. W. Ottoson, ed., *Land Use Policy*, 3, 24.

54. Johnson, "Misconceptions," 391.

55. D. K. Weisberg, "Barred from the Bar: Women and Legal Education in the United States, 1870–1890," *Journal of Legal Education* 28 (1977): 485.

56. Janeway, review of Carroll Smith-Rosenberg, *Disorderly Conduct: Visions of Gender in Victorian America* (1985), in *New York Times Book Review*, Aug. 25, 1985, 11; Barbara M. Solomon, *In the Company of Educated Women* (1985).

57. Interview, Mrs. Hobby with author, Houston, Tex., 1969; on Bascom and Gregory, Lois B. Arnold, *Four Lives in Science: Women's Education in the Nineteenth Century* (1985).

58. Sandoz, "The Homestead in Perspective," in Ottoson, ed., *Land Use Policy*, 47, 62.

59. Sklar, "Florence Kelley and the Women's World of Progressive Reform," (Paper delivered to annual meeting of the Organization of American Historians, 1984); Margaret Rossiter, "Doctorates for American Women, 1868–1907," *History of Education Quarterly* 22 (1982): 159; Joan Hawks, "Lady Legislators: The Southern Experience," (Paper delivered to annual meeting of the American Historical Association, 1985).

60. W. E. B. Du Bois, *Against Racism: Unpublished Essays, Papers, Addresses, 1887–1961*, ed. H. Aptheker (1985), quoted in N. Huggins's review in *New York Times Book Review*, Sept. 30, 1985, 25.

61. Donald Nieman, "Black Ballot Power and Republican Justice: The Impact of Black Political Power on the Administration of Justice in the Reconstruction South," (Paper delivered at Symposium on Emancipation and Its Aftermath, City University of New York, 1983).

62. S. M. Shannon, "Land-Grant College Legislation and Black Tennesseans," *History of Education Quarterly* 2 (1982): 139.

Chapter 3. The 1944 G.I. Bill

1. Davis R. B. Ross, *Preparing for Ulysses: Politics and Veterans During World War II* (1969), 123.

2. Eleanor Roosevelt quoted in Geoffrey C. Ward, *Before the Trumpet: Young Franklin Roosevelt, 1882–1905* (1985), 6; Stiles in Berkhofer, "Providing for the Expansion of a Republican Empire: From Jefferson's Ordinance of 1784 to the Northwest Ordinance of 1787" (Paper delivered to annual meeting of the Organization of American Historians, 1968), 5.

3. Dixon Wecter, *When Johnny Comes Marching Home* (1944), pt. 1, chap. 6; pt. 2, chaps. 7–8; pt. 3, chap. 9.

4. In Samuel I. Rosenman, ed., *Public Papers and Addresses of Franklin D. Roosevelt, (1938–50)*, 13 vols., 2: 375–76.

5. Wecter, *When Johnny Comes Marching Home*, 549, errs on the point of novelty, by forgetting the Morrill and Homestead Acts.

6. W. Form, *Divided We Stand: Working-Class Stratification in America* (1985).

7. R. S. McElvaine, "Workers in Fiction: Locked Out," *New York Times Book Review*, Sept. 1, 1985, 1, 19; Irving Howe, *Socialism and America* (1985).

8. Ross, *Preparing for Ulysses*, esp. chap. 4; Danial D. Luria, "Wealth, Capital, and Power: The Social Meaning of Home Ownership," *Journal of Interdisciplinary History* 7 (Autumn 1976): 261.

9. S. Kesselman, *Modernization of American Reform* (1979), chaps. 8, 9, conclusion.

10. J. Anthony Lukas, *Common Ground: A Turbulent Decade in the Lives of Three American Families* (1985).

11. Ryan, *Cradle of the Middle Class* (1981), xiii, 13.

12. Jensen, "Quantitative Collective Biography," in R. Swierenga, ed., *Quantification in American History* (1970), 389; Daniel Coleman, "The Psyche of the Entrepreneur," *New York Times Magazine*, Feb. 2, 1986, 30–33, 59.

13. Bledstein, *The Culture of Professionalism: The Middle Class and the Development of Higher Education in America* (1976), 334, passim.

14. Bensen, "Group Cohesion and Social and Ideological Conflict," *American Behavioral Scientist* 16 (1973): 741; R. Berthoff, *An Unsettled People: Social Order and Disorder in American History* (1971); G. Pierson, "A Restless Temper," *American Historical Review* 69 (1964), 969.

15. Blumin, "The Hypothesis of Middle-Class Formulation in Nineteenth Century America," *American Historical Review* 90 (1985), 299, 336–37. David O. Levine, *The American College and the Culture of Aspiration, 1915–1940* (1986) suggests that America was ambivalent

about democracy as reflected in the growth here of a differentiated system of higher education, one in which elite classes preserved their prerogatives in Ivy colleges and universities while, in relative terms, the "masses" resorted to the tax-supported institutions in order to achieve economic and social mobility. Professor Levine was kind enough to afford me insights into his forthcoming book, as well as a copy of his 1985 American Historical Association paper, "Is Higher Education a Privilege or a Right?"

16. Cf. R. K. Murray, *Red Scare: A Study in National Hysteria, 1919–1920* (1955), and D. E. Carleton, *Red Scare! Right-Wing Hysteria, Fifties Fanaticism, and Their Legacy in Texas* (1985).

17. C. B. Nam, "Impact of the 'G.I. Bills' on the Educational Level of the Male Population," *Social Forces* 43 (1964): 26, 32; Keith Olson, "The GI Bill and Higher Education: Success and Surprise," *American Quarterly* 25 (1973): 596; Nam, *The GI Bill, the Veterans, and the Colleges* (1974).

18. J. R. Emmens, "Education Begets Education: The GI Bill Twenty Years Later," *American Education* 1 (1965): 13.

19. S. M. Shannon, "Land-Grant College Legislation and Black Tennesseans," *History of Education Quarterly* 2 (1982): 139; John and Ruth Wennersten, "Separate and Unequal: The Evolution of a Black Land Grant College in Maryland," *Maryland Historical Magazine* 72 (1977): 110; Dwight O. W. Holmes, *The Evolution of the Negro College* (1934).

20. Bert Haigh, *Land, Oil, and Education* (1984).

21. Fred Mathews, "The Reassertion of American Exceptionalism: From Progressivism to Liberalism in the Intellectual Weeklies, 1920–1950" (Paper delivered to annual meeting of the Southern Historical Association, 1985); Matusow, *The Unraveling of America: A History of Liberalism in the 1960s* (1984); Clecak, *America's Quest for the Ideal Self: Dissent and Fulfillment in the 60s and 70s* (1985); Chafe, *The Unfinished Journey: America Since World War II* (1985).

22. Maeroff, "After Twenty Years," *New York Times*, Sept. 30, 1985, Y 11; Rathje, "A Decent Burial," *The Atlantic*, Sept. 1985, 16, 18.

23. Alonzo Hamby, *Liberalism and Its Challengers* (1985).

Index